AMERICAN
DIVA

ALSO BY DEBORAH PAREDEZ

Year of the Dog

*Selenidad: Selena, Latinos, and
the Performance of Memory*

This Side of Skin

AMERICAN DIVA

Extraordinary,

Unruly,

Fabulous

———

Deborah Paredez

W. W. NORTON & COMPANY
Independent Publishers Since 1923

For information about permission to reproduce
selections from this book, write to Permissions,
W. W. Norton & Company, Inc.
500 Fifth Avenue, New York, NY 10110

For information about special discounts for bulk purchases,
please contact W. W. Norton Special Sales at
specialsales@wwnorton.com or 800-233-4830

Manufacturing by Lake Book Manufacturing
Book design by Buckley Design
Production manager: Lauren Abbate

ISBN 978-1-324-03530-5

W. W. Norton & Company, Inc.
500 Fifth Avenue, New York, N.Y. 10110

www.wwnorton.com

W. W. Norton & Company Ltd.
15 Carlisle Street, London W1D 3BS

1 2 3 4 5 6 7 8 9 0

For Lucia M. Bustillo

Contents

————

x CONTENTS

AMERICAN DIVA

Vikki Carr's Voice

The sound of a diva's voice was how I knew we were Mexican. Or, at least, how I knew we couldn't hide it from the neighbors. My earliest childhood memories are suffused with the sounds of Vikki Carr's contralto rising from my father's turntable, spinning out past the flimsy screens. Her voice a swath of silk turned out, a *bandera* unfurled from the window.

In the spring of 1973, driven by his own immigrant aspiration and the Walter Younger–inspired dreams that emerged in those early years of desegregation, my father decided to move our family from the south side ("Mexican") to the north side ("white") of San Antonio. We landed in a newly built neighborhood of modest, one-car-garage homes that rimmed the outermost edge of a "good" public school district filled at its center with more spacious two-car-garage houses. We lived on that border.

Before our move north, we had lived on a street punctuated on both ends by properties owned by my maternal great-grandparents: the "Bustillo Drive-In Grocery and Ice House"

1

(think bodega crossed with juke joint) and a two-room house that my parents rented in the first years after they married. Nearly every house or vacant lot lining the street in between these points was owned or inhabited by someone to whom I was related by blood or marriage or habit. One long family line.

I don't remember that first house or the countless times it flooded or the storm that soaked through the roof ruining my father's prized collection of LPs and reel-to-reels and some of his stereo equipment, the flood that led him soon after to cross the tracks and drive the long stretch of highway across town to sign a loan and make a down payment on a thirty-year mortgage.

What I do remember is spending my earliest years at the ice house among extended family and the weekend regulars who'd lay down the burdens of their workweek over beers and card games or the latest Avon catalogues. There are more

Dancing on the tabletop

than a few family stories and snapshots of me as a toddler poised on a tabletop alongside half-empty bottles and discarded poker hands, surrounded by kinfolk all cheering on my efforts at dancing. Always in the background, blurry but visible: the jukebox that played accordion-driven conjuntos or the crooning harmonies of doo-wop or the plaintive longings of Vikki Carr.

Florencia Bisenta de Casillas-Martinez Cardona was born along the border in El Paso, Texas, in 1941 and became Vikki Carr somewhere along the way to recording artist fame, most notably for her soaring 1967 ballad, "It Must Be Him." Legions of English-speaking fans from my parents' and grandparents' generations knew her as the classy songbird praised by Ethel Merman for her *tremendous talent* in the liner notes of Carr's 1965 album, *Anatomy of Love*, and by Dean Martin who called her *the best girl singer in the business*. But, back then, in the early to mid-1970s, only a few of us were listening to her in Spanish.

In the midst of her English-language success and not long after signing with Columbia Records in 1970, Carr convinced Clive Davis to produce a Spanish-language album, *Vikki Carr En Español*, in 1972—a move that long predated the return-to-roots crossover endeavors of other Latin music divas like Linda Ronstadt and Gloria Estefan. This was also before, as Carr recounts, Clive Davis informed her, "*I can only work with one diva at a time, and I have two.*" *So he dropped me. And stayed with Barbra [Streisand].*

Of course, I didn't know any of this back in the mid-1970s when I was just starting elementary school, one of the few brown faces warming the pale tint of the class photos. Despite my auspicious ice-house beginnings, I was now learning to leave behind any aspirations to stand on tabletops, any impulse to stand out at all. Well-meaning teachers praised my well-behaved, bookish manner, calling out my name in roll call, having long ignored the accent that was supposed to accompany the first "e" in the correct Spanish spelling of my name—/PAIR–uh–deez?/ or / PURR-ah-dehz?/—or forego-ing one syllable altogether—/Perez/—before finally just set-tling on *Parades* (as in "Don't Rain on My . . .") or *Paradise*, a surname I could only have earned had I not let go of my table-dancing dreams.

What I did know in these years was that when my father laid the needle down on the lead track—a plangent song called "Y volveré"—Carr would pull us in with her whispered vale-diction, *Amor adios*, and pull us out toward the swell of her overwrought command to suffer no more. The song dwelling in the moment of departure, reckoning with the end of love and the beginning of what comes after. A resignation toward solitude and a promise of return as the title suggests. I could not yet translate its meaning; for me as for many Mexican-American kids my age, Spanish was the language parents spoke to keep secrets from the children or on phone conver-sations with grandparents. I could not yet hear the assurances offered by its future tense.

Carr's voice was clear and pure and resonant, a struck bell meant to be heard from across a great distance. Or at least across the street. Her voice turned up to a volume that exposed us to others. A voice heard all along the block by trim white moth-ers who sat around kitchen tables ashing their Salems. A voice that carried three doors down where the Irish Catholic family ate cheese sandwiches cut into right angles or up the block where until the 1980s the only other brown family lived. A voice I knew the neighbors could hear. A voice announcing our difference. We were Mexican. We were the ones who turned up the music and put dancing toddlers on tables and unfolded lawn chairs on the oil-stained driveway while her voice spilled out its longings, its insistence on a brighter tomorrow, *Quizás mañana brille el sol*. We stayed outside past twilight. We turned the record over and played the other side. We knew both sides.

We were Mexican. I was mortified. And I was mesmerized. Because, I mean, how could I not eventually surrender to that voice and those unabashed orchestrations supporting it? Her voice as virtuous as a telenovela maid. The strings so lush so fulsome so deliberate so deliberately sentimental. So Mexican. The melodrama of it all! I was at once drawn inside the cleared hollow made by her voice and deafened by its pealing truths: a beast inside the bell tower, I was filled with wonder and with shame, teeth shuddering from each strike. Her voice was irrefutable proof and proclamation of our Mexicanness. I cowered in its echo and I made it my home.

The sound of a diva's voice was how I came to know my place in relation to others in the neighborhood. Which is to say how I came to know my place in relation to Americanness. In relation to others like me who are rarely invited to join the choruses of America's anthems. But, divas help us, too, sing America. Or, as Rita Moreno once famously sang, *América*. The diva's voice is the bell struck and the alarm sounded, the call for gathering and the call for escape. It is, as well, the very destination—the holy place or the other-place—to which her voice leads. The sound of a thing and the thing itself.

A diva is often known for the ravishing power of her voice. And, sometimes, for its tragic ravishment. Her voice is the source of her authority and her vulnerability. She contradicts herself, she is large, she contains multitudes. She holds a note and carries within it all of our dreaming and damaged and glorious and gutted bodies. Divas inspire those of us devoted to them to train our voices likewise, toward the achievement of capaciousness, of maximalist flourish, of more is more, and all of our outrageous overmuchness. To be the sound of the thing and the thing itself.

The sound of a diva's voice is sometimes all we need to lead us through or to lead us out. And sometimes, the sound of a diva's voice is what leads us back. Returns us to the long-forgotten flooded house, the house flooded with the sounds of a woman's woe and resilience. Vikki Carr repeats the refrain, *"Y volveré."* Listening again to the song, I am struck by the way it ends, by the way its fade-out resists an ending, refuses closure. The fade-out, a common practice for popular tunes of its day, certainly situates the song in a particular soundscape of the early 1970s. But the volume diminishing on Carr's voice as it crests with her promise of return as a bird in flight also suggests a defiance of time, a sense of the infinite. She has, perhaps, been singing all along, her voice carrying across a great distance.

Listen again with me now. I'm at long last able to translate the lyrics. Can you hear Carr sing about waiting for her lover's return? On the surface, it sounds like rather standard lost-love song sentiment, her insistence on keeping, as she sings in Spanish, your light shining on my path. But let's listen again. Can you hear it? Can you see it? I find myself lingering on that line, on that light, and I am overcome by a sense of synesthesia. I blink dumbly at the illumination emanating from the sound of her voice. She keeps singing, and her voice is the illuminated path. All I need to do is follow her.

Diva Definitions

Me and Ms. (Grace) Jones

I was born the year thousands of women marched down Fifth Avenue and rallied in Bryant Park for the 1970 Women's Strike for Equality. The year that farther uptown, Iris Morales joined other young Nuyorican freedom fighters to form the Women's Caucus in the New York chapter of the Young Lords Party. It was the year that Nina Simone released the civil rights anthem "To Be Young, Gifted and Black," inspired by Lorraine Hansberry's autobiographical play. The year Angela Davis was captured by the FBI in New York City and extradited to California, to await trial in a Marin County jail cell. I was born during her imprisonment. It was the year Vikki Carr, with her silky contralto spun from her borderlands roots, was named "Woman of the Year" by the *Los Angeles Times*. The year Chicana activist Gloria Arellanes joined 30,000 others in Los Angeles for the Chicano Moratorium, one of the largest anti-war protests in the nation's history. The year Tina Turner premiered her (and Ike's) version of "Proud Mary" on the *Ed Sullivan Show*, all husk and horns and shimmy and soul and gold fringe flying. The year Diana Ross left the Supremes and Audre Lorde came out in her poem "Martha," declaring, *We shall love each other here if ever at all.* A time marked by so many freedom movements, by bold acts demonstrating new ways of modeling freedom of movement. I was born and began to move within the spaces made by these women who marched and wrote and sang and shouted and strutted across the stage and the street and often in the margins. I was born in the fringe—the gold and shimmering fringe—they made for so many like me.

I was born and reborn from all of these political and cultural movements, by the singular and collective acts of these women. From an early age, I was drawn to strong, complicated, virtuosic, larger-than-life, unruly women who variously referred to themselves or each other as *girlfriend* or *mujer* or *comrade* or *sister* or *hermana* or *gurl* or simply by an iconic first name. I preferred to call them, with love and admiration, divas. Women who could fill every corner of the room with their voices or their fierceness or their desires or their visions or their attitudes or their shoe collection. As a child, I delighted in Diana Ross in *The Wiz* and Miss Piggy's outsized appetites and Lena Horne on *Sesame Street* affirming "It's Not Easy Bein' Green." As a teen, I wrote poems inspired by Medea and Circe of ancient Greece (tragic classical divas, for sure) and marveled at the tear-soaked voices of the Mexican bolero singers (more tragic classical divas) that rose from my father's turntable.

Which makes me of a certain age. Which makes me troubled sometimes by the ways we've filled up or emptied out categories like feminism or freedom or diva in the decades since my birth. Which makes me second-wave and third-world and ¡Si Se Puede! and *Sister Outsider* and fist-raised and "Free Angela" and *Free to Be You and Me* and Rita Moreno's rooftop mambo and Labelle's "Lady Marmalade" and Dolly and Lily and Jane working *Nine to Five* and "Bidi Bidi Bom Bom" and "Bemba Colorá" and *Hey blue, there is a song for you* and "Blue Bayou" and Broadway-baby and in love with women who lash at you with their belting voices, women who don't just take to the stage, but overtake it. Who leave you wrecked and ready to revolt.

Which is to say that I've long been training to be a feminist performance critic who's enthralled by the relationship between divas and feminism and other freedom movements. I want to know why and how exactly divas have sustained me and so many like me—the brown, the freaks, the feminists, the thespians rarely cast in the lead, the awkward and crooked-teethed, the otherwise shy, the poets—the ones Gloria Anzaldúa once described as *the atravesados, the squint-eyed, the perverse, the queer, the troublesome, the mongrel, the mulatto, the half-breed, the half-dead.* I'm interested in how divas have changed and how they've changed me over the last fifty years. I want to make sense of the tremendous proliferation and transformation of the word "diva" during the course of my lifetime into a term of derision for women who make demands or into a role of aspiration for youngsters attempting to define and navigate the terrain of girlhood. I want to know how and why divas, once synonymous with virtuosity, became symbols of vitriol. And how and why, through it all, I've kept on loving them.

Divas have played leading roles in my formation as a female artist, feminist critic, and fan of formidable and fearsome women. Divas and diva adoration have shaped my critical preoccupations, my poetic sensibilities, my feminist consciousness, my female friendships, my approach to motherhood, and my unabashed love of musicals. Above all, loving divas in all of their virtuosity and all of their unruliness has fostered my love for all the virtuosic and unruly women around me. For even as the diva is revered and reviled for her stubborn singularity, even as she insists on standing alone in the spotlight, even as she throws shade and tantrums, she has taught me not to fear or feel threatened by messy and marvelous women, but to be in marvelous and messy relation to them. What's more feminist and fabulous and fearsome than that?

This is a story of how divas have helped me become a brown feminist writer, artist, and mother of a certain age. A story of how divas have modeled for me how to love, raise, and write about strong, complicated, imperfect, virtuosic women who last and last and last. The divas who accompany me here—just a small sampling of my diva pantheon—include popular figures from film, television, opera, music, sports, and the stage. To tell my story is to tell the story of my diva relations: Vikki Carr, Grace Jones, Rita Moreno, Tina Turner, Divine, Aretha Franklin, Celia Cruz, La India, Selena, Serena and Venus Williams, Jomama Jones, Patti LaBelle, Nona Hendryx, Sarah Dash, and Nadine Sierra. Oh, and my great-aunt, Lucia Bustillo, because what would a book about divas be without the inclusion of an influential, eccentric auntie? And, of course, there are beloved others who didn't make their way into these pages, but aren't divas known for the ways they escape the confines of whatever seeks to contain them? While the divas included here may hail from different mediums and moments in time, they all share starring roles in guiding a brown girl—by song or by serve, by style or by swerve—a little closer to freedom.

Divas have shaped American ideas about feminism, free market principles, and freedom struggles during the last fifty years. Along the way, divas have cleared spaces for me to think and write and sing and shout and dream and grieve. Even as she is vilified, the diva has remained a constant presence in my life and in the larger cultural imagination over the last half century. Perhaps this is because divas give voice to and amplify that very American concept of freedom. Divas and our devotion to them have helped so many of us—especially those of us relegated to the margins—in our strivings to know, as Nina Simone once sang, *how it feels to be free*. And just like the idea of freedom in America, founded as it is on the bondage of others, divas are rife with contradictions. In their increasingly iconic status as singular and lucrative brands, divas have played a starring role in promoting "free market" principles. In this way, divas offer at once liberating expressions of power or desire or community and more troubling ideas of unfettered commodification. My life has spanned this evolution (devolution) of the diva—which makes me want to turn back over the past half century, to turn the record over and play the B side, to turn up the volume and tune in to all the sounds that divas make.

I was born the year Grace Jones—pop singer, actress, style icon, performance artist, trickster figure, disco diva—moved to Paris and quickly became a model and muse for fashion designers like Issey Miyake and fashion illustrators like Antonio Lopez. It was not long after she had shaved her head for the first time and began to shape what would become her signature Afro-alien androgynous look. *It made me look hard in a soft world*, Jones recalls. She returned from Paris and became a fixture in New York City's gay disco nightclubs like the Paradise Garage and the star-studded Studio 54. In the 1970s and 1980s, she recorded albums pulsing with enduring disco dance club hits ("Pull Up to the Bumper" and "I Need a Man") and reggae-infused new wave songs ("Warm Leatherette") and was nominated for a 1984 "Best Long Form Video" Grammy Award for her performance-art-meets-concert-montage, "One Man Show." On film, she played up her machine-meets-mantis-meets-menace persona as villain to James Bond and Conan the Destroyer and transformed herself into a red-haired vampire in head-to-toe body paint in geometric patterns created and applied by Keith Haring. She's been called controversial and confrontational, transmasculine and a sexy genderfuck, robot and raunch, alien and alienating, a hologram and a hurricane, a question mark followed by an exclamation point, timeless and time-traveling, a deviant and a diva. In 2012, at 64 years old, she stole the show at the Queen of England's Diamond Jubilee concert, when she hula-hooped in a shiny red-and-black leotard for the entire four-minute-long performance of her 1985 hit, "Slave to the Rhythm." Grace Jones may have been born in Jamaica, but really she's from another dimension.

I was born, Grace Jones begins the first chapter of her memoir, *It happened one day, when I least expected it.* She was born. And yet, she speaks of her arrival as if she preceded it and was already preoccupied with other matters. She least expected it. *The diva hasn't yet arrived at herself,* the poet and diva devotee Wayne Koestenbaum reminds us, *she is in a continual, gratifying state of becoming.* The diva: epic, always in *medias res.* Or as Jones says, *I am always becoming something. I am always turning into something else.*

The diva—as the embodiment of an unapologetically fierce, preternaturally gifted and charismatic, gender-troubling female (or outrageously feminine) performer—has long been an enduring object of reverence and revulsion. Sarah Bernhardt basked in twenty-seven curtain calls during the 1880 New York premiere of her American tour while garnering the derision of "respectable society" for her uncorseted body and lifestyle; Josephine Baker wowed and scandalized Parisian audiences in 1926 with her undulating banana skirt; and Yoko Ono literally cut a swath through conceptual art with her 1964 performance, "Cut Piece," and then went on, according to many, to break up the Beatles. The diva is divine redeemer and sublime demon. Utterly human in all of her public trials and superhuman in her performative virtuosity and posthuman in all of her glorious gender fuckery and wardrobe arsenal. Earthly flesh and supernatural force. *I looked natural and unnatural at the same time*, Grace Jones describes herself. She is glamorous and monstrous, an empowering female public figure and a catty bitch behind the scenes. Divas may share many of the characteristics of modern celebrities—a broad fan base, a status of distinctive singularity, a public persona haunted by the roles they've made famous—but their virtuosity, charisma, resiliency, and capacity for reinvention set divas apart from other stars.

The origins of the term "diva" can be traced back to "Casta diva" (Chaste Goddess), an 1831 aria from Bellini's opera *Norma*. While the term was once reserved for virtuosic female opera sopranos, "diva" has evolved over the course of the late twentieth and early twenty-first centuries to refer, often derisively, to a female public figure who displays a haughty attitude accompanied only sometimes by a masterful skill. Over this long duration, divas have endured as repositories for our fantasies and anxieties about the pleasures and risks of unapologetically powerful women who move with finesse or with force (and often with both) through the public sphere. A diva's voice defies the laws of gravity. Her very excess—the makeup! the wardrobe! the high notes! the chutzpah!—offers a capacious space wherein we create ourselves or condemn the worlds that seek to constrain us.

The diva is a force of—or against—nature. Natural and unnatural at the same time, she sustains contradictions. *I am rooted and restless*, Jones tells us, *I am at peace, but I want to interrupt.* She is singing just for me and she is aloof. She can feed your soul and she can eat you alive. She can keep us rolling on the river, but, as Tina Turner warns us, she won't get us there nice and easy, but nice and rough. She is all sweat and shout and shrug and show show show. *My shaved head made me look more abstract*, Jones recalls, *less tied to a specific race or sex or tribe, but also a way of moving across those things, belonging while at the same time not belonging.* This is the diva dialectic: proximity and distance, effortlessness and discipline, salvation and ravishment.

Sometimes the diva asserts herself as at once consummately feminine and excessively defiant of its bounds. Other times, she is, as Jones sings in "Walking in the Rain," *Feeling like a woman, looking like a man / Sounding like a "no-no."* Because of this gender blurring, a diva is often hailed as a queer icon and a queering force. Music critic Francesca Royster swoons over Grace Jones: *I recognized in her thrilling contrariness, her "Feeling like a No-No," a female masculine home girl.* The diva is the floodgate, unlatched. She's the deluge. Koestenbaum declares, *A diva is said to* come out *from behind the curtains for her bows. When we see a diva she is, by definition, out.* She voices our outcries. She is outlaw, she is outlandish, she is outrageous, and when she is outraged, her wrath rends dressing rooms to rubble. She is doing it all out in public. The diva, it seems, is always performing, always playing (at) herself, obliterating the distinction between private and public, authenticity and artifice, feeling like a woman and looking like a man. *My life*, Jones declares, *is out there.*

When Grace Jones released her second studio album, *Fame*, in 1978, she celebrated its release and her thirtieth birthday with fellow divas Divine and Nona Hendryx and a nightclub full of friends and fans at the Xenon disco in New York City. At one point during that dazzlingly hedonistic night, Jones, dressed as the Egyptian queen Nefertiti, straddled a motorcycle along with Hendryx (and a dog-collared dancer sandwiched between them) while extending her hand down to feed birthday cake to Divine, who was stretched out on the floor, mouth opened wide. Jones would later recall this particular scene as *a frenzied fantasy world I felt very at home in.* The photos from the party pulse with the sybaritic splendor of bodies pressed ass to pelvis, breasts to back, thigh to thigh taking turns atop the bike while Divine stretches out on a bed of crushed carnations. So

Happy Birthday, Grace Jones

much glint and gleam—metallic eyeshadow, dog-collar studs, linked chains on a dancer's G-string, gold-strapped high heels, the cycle's chrome. Rosy hues streaked across each tableau— Jones's scarlet-lacquered nails, Divine's carmine minidress and rouged cheeks, the machine's shiny red fuel tank, slices of pink cake and flashes of pink tongues and pink carnations strewn among the white ones, so many perfectly lined ver- million lips. All the bodies glistening and so fully inhabited. In one shot, they are holding wedges of cake; in another, they are licking the icing off their fingers. In one frame, a dancer's arm is hooked under Hendryx's leg; in another, Jones stretches her arms in a wide V holding out the corners of her headscarf and exposing the small patch of hair in her armpit. So much deliriously exposed: a dancer's tan line along his left pelvis, the inseam of Hendryx's white bodysuit as she spreads open her legs, the hair on the toes of another dancer's bare feet, Divine's panties and a splash of sweat on her snarling face, Jones's shaved thigh as hard and slick as a strip of onyx. The scenes are all palm and crotch and mouth and *wait, whose arm is that?* Every part of every body open and hungry for more and more. The exhilarating polymorphous perversity of it all.

A diva teaches us how to indulge our wildest appetites, how to prostrate ourselves to our wants and demand they be met. She revs the engine of her desires and invites us all along for the ride. Her transgressions and her risk-taking and her outrageous excess lead her and those of us who dance to her music or dive into the roiling depths of her voice toward pleasure and more pleasure: *Shaving my head led directly to my first orgasm*, Jones declares. The diva insists on pleasure as a way of knowing and enduring. She offers lessons about the reparative work of feeling good for bodies that have been historically marked by suffering or shame: *I was preaching pleasure as a certain sort of threat*. Pleasure as a threat to those who would rather we lie prostrate to our pain or before the altar of ordinariness. And threat as an inherent dimension to pleasure; threat to the status quo, threat to the borders that have been erected to divide us from one another and from our own radiant wants.

Divas and their training return us again and again to the body. A diva's training says, *Watch me descend into the cavernous recesses of my body and watch me ascend with the treasures I've mined there and now watch me transcend the body's earthbound destinies*. A diva's virtuosity is often marked by a capacious (and rapacious) approach to embodiment and by her ability to blast through the body's apparent limits and long-held wounds: the impossibly elongated extension of Rita Moreno's high kick, Donna Summer's ecstatic, 16-minute-long "Love to Love You Baby" unfurled on the dance floor, Celia Cruz's verbal dexterity and molten contralto, the rigorous conditioning of 71-year-old Cher's five-minute planks, the android angularity of Grace

Jones. Divas teach us about discipline in the service of bodily triumph and transgressions: *In my own way,* Jones reflects, *I am very militant and disciplined. Even if that sometimes means being militantly naughty, and disciplined in the arts of subversion.*

Among her many powers, a diva has staying power. She lasts and lasts and makes a discipline out of outlasting her detractors or even time itself. As a result, divas know a thing or two about the comeback, about the second (or third or thousandth) coming, about the promise of tomorrow. *My instincts were to become someone else, to be unbound, to be born once more,* Jones writes, *I was born. I will be born.* Tina Turner was reborn in her diva comeback with the release of "Private Dancer" in May 1984 as I was nearing the end of seventh grade. I had just discovered poetry and that I loved to write it and was spending much of my time at home curled up in my bedroom reading poems through my smudged glasses. But, sometimes, when my parents weren't home and my brother was out reenacting Evel Knievel stunts on his bike (which was often, Generation X latchkey kids that we were), I would slip the album from its sleeve and drop the needle down and do my own private dancing. I'd sing along to no one in particular and everyone everywhere, ventriloquizing Tina's spiked-hair-and-heels demand, *You'd better be good to me.* I was rehearsing my own arrival through the voice and gestures of the diva's return.

Divas are simultaneously of their time and timeless. They make an art out of keeping a finger on the pulse of our needs and desires in the here and now while also transporting us from our wearied, pulsing bodies toward an elsewhere beyond the confines of the present. Indeed, a diva's legitimacy is often measured not simply by her ability to capture the zeitgeist of her times but by her transcendence of it. The diva lifts us beyond the confines of the present, beyond the limits of straight time. The diva does not need to start on time because she is out of time. *I am in three or four time zones at the same time*, Jones insists. And she is in time. In time with fashion. In time with ferocity. In time with feeling. In time with the baseline of her desires. And she is ahead of her time. Refusing the right now in her insistence that it's time for what's next. The diva is not just present tense, but subjunctive. Not simply in time with what is, but with what ought to have been, what ought to be.

The diva shamelessly insists that the spotlight shine on her darkness. She often inspires our devotion not simply because of the ways she is like us, but because of the ways she shows us how to draw upon her difference as the very source of her power. It's no wonder that those of us living on the social margins often turn to the diva as a guide for how to live along the fault lines that threaten our daily living. She's marked by difference itself, *a witch with a smear of blood on my cheek*, Jones insists. She is Other, she is Other-wise. Not unlike so many of us who worship her, the diva is often cast outside the boundaries of the normal, the human, the pure, the pretty, the pallor of whiteness. Her darkness is, of course, racialized, her bad behavior and ungovernable demeanor often conflated with and attributed to her darkness.

But for all of this racial othering, Black women have historically been excluded from the exalted category of the disciplined, virtuosic diva even as they are regularly disregarded—which is to say racialized—as excessive and demanding and monstrous divas. Extraordinary Black female performers—from Bessie Smith to Billie Holiday to Nina Simone to Aretha Franklin— were often characterized by their "natural" talents or "unnatural" appetites rather than acknowledged for the extraordinary training and discipline they modeled and the daily barrage of diminishment they endured. Natural and unnatural at the same time. But, as Black feminist music scholars like Farah Jasmine Griffin and Daphne Brooks remind us, it is precisely this long line of Black divas who have taught us the most about how to get free. Griffin writes about how the singing Black woman is regularly summoned as a spectacle of healing in times of national crisis while she is simultaneously denied rights within the nation. Part of the Black diva's extraordinary skill, Griffin writes, is her ability to train her voice to travel in frequencies beyond this deployment, audible to Black Americans in their own freedom struggles. *Black women's singing*, Griffin writes, *has articulated our most heartfelt political, social, spiritual, and romantic longings and in so doing has given us a sense of ourselves as a people beyond the confines of our oppression.* Brooks writes about the *many registers* in which Black divas have sung *the core meaning and vision of liberation itself.* Sometimes that freedom sounds like a slap across a cheek and sometimes it looks like a blood-smeared cheek and other times it feels like cheeks flushed with so much life-affirming heat.

The diva *has a loud voice in a public world*, diva scholars Susan Leonardi and Rebecca Pope proclaim in *The Diva's Mouth*, and, as such, her voice *is a political force.* Opera impresario Matthew Epstein once quipped, *In a funny way, the emergence of the diva was a beginning of women's liberation* due largely to the ways she commands the stage with her virtuosity and audacity and makes us submit to her. In one of her most iconic interviews, Jones slapped (and slapped and slapped) her white, male interviewer, Russell Harty, during his BBC talk show in response to his dismissive and rude treatment of her. The diva—and the Black diva, in particular—reminds us that no matter her position, the world will seek to diminish her. She shows us how to strike back against this daily diminishment. But, despite her position as a powerful and unapologetically ambitious and accomplished woman, the diva is, nonetheless, not always a friend of feminism. Her insistent singularity, her outsider pose, her competitiveness with other divas, her effortlessly executed side-eye, all make her relationship with a collective cause vexed, at best. In the

end, she refuses to be fixed within the category of empowering role model for unruly women.

And yet. . . . Angela Davis turns to the sounds of blues
queens to expand our understandings of Black feminism. *What
can we learn from women like Gertrude "Ma" Rainey, Bessie Smith,
and Billie Holiday,* Davis asks, *that we may not be able to learn
from Ida B. Wells, Anna Julia Cooper, and Mary Church Terrell?*
She listens closely to the scratched recordings of their voices,
lifting and dropping the needle again and again and again to
transcribe their lyrics and translate their inflections, to hear
in their songs the otherwise muted articulations of Black
working-class feminist consciousness. She tunes our ears to
hear the blues diva's unabashed and repeated pronouncements
of female desire, to hear in these assertions the audacious ways
sexuality is not privatized in the blues. The blues queen's life turns
our insides out. And this, Davis shows us, is precisely the path
toward freedom. Bessie Smith's voice resounds against the violence depicted in her "Downhearted Blues" to assert in her
concluding lyrics, *I got the world in a jug, the stopper's in my hand
/ I'm gonna hold it until you men come under my command.* Her
voice carrying the weight of her struggle; her voice, the vessel
that carries her through. The needle drops to the groove and
she rasps and wails and we rise toward the surface of our refusals, our demands, our desires.

I was born the year Janis Joplin collaborated with Juanita
Green, then president of the North Philadelphia chapter of
the NAACP, to pay for a long-overdue headstone for Bessie
Smith's unmarked grave. They chose the epitaph: *The Greatest Blues Singer in the World Will Never Stop Singing.* Janis had
honed the rasp and gut in her voice by listening to Bessie
Smith albums over and over and trying to imitate her sound.
She showed me the air, Janis once said of Smith, *and taught me
how to fill it.* Some say Janis believed, with the guileless arrogance only a white girl could have, that she was, in fact, Smith

reincarnated. Green, on the other hand, credited the Empress of the Blues for steering her clear of the stage and toward an education and an eventual nursing degree. As a girl, Green had worked as a domestic for Smith; once after hearing Green sing, Bessie asked, *Is you in school? Well, you better stay there 'cause you can't carry a note.* I wonder about Juanita Green, about all the other ways she followed the sound of Bessie Smith's voice.

I sang along to Janis Joplin's version of "Me and Bobby McGee" with my friend Nicole in a nice and rough a cappella throughout high school. We sang together backstage or in dressing rooms or on long bus rides to out-of-town thespian tournaments. We didn't yet know much about freedom or even about the constraints against it that produced the very blues to which Janis was aspiring. What we did know is that we wanted, like Janis had, to ride out to New Orleans, to be free of Texas, to be free of the petty dramas of adolescence. We knew it wasn't really about the lyrics, anyway, but about the ride out, about our voices meeting in the empty air, about filling it with the sound of our longing. We sang *freedom's just another word for nothin' left to lose* not yet knowing that what Janis was wanting wasn't freedom but reunion with the one who got away. We sang and sang and sang and, in our singing, we experienced the tenderness and intensity—the erotics—that girlhood friendship forged. Sometimes a diva gives us the anthem we rehearse with another to feel our sense of belonging, to feel our way free. *Feeling good was good enough for me.*

Divas have a way of taking ownership, of laying claim to that which is not readily (if ever) given to them. Sometimes the diva's act of possession is the coup we've all been waiting for. Those times when she lays claim enough to convince you and everyone that whatever it is she has seized has belonged to her all along. A diva doesn't just cover a song; she makes it hers. The way Janis blued and scuffed The Chantels' doo-wop version of "Maybe." The way Tina Turner roughed up Credence Clearwater Revival's "Proud Mary." The way the Queen of Soul, Aretha Franklin, sang Carole King's "(You Make Me Feel Like) A Natural Woman." The way she performed it at the Kennedy Center in 2015 to "honor" King. The way she walked onstage still carrying her coat and purse, as if to say, "Oh, I've just arrived, and, oh, really, you'd like me to sing a little something? Well, maybe just this once." The way she set her sequined clutch atop the piano and played the hell out of that song while still wearing her floor-length fur. The way she brought President Obama to tears with just the sound of her voice. The way she stood mid-song and made us all submit to her, the way she took off her coat and let it fall as she lifted off from the lyrics on *I feel like I feel like aaaah aaahh aaahh*. The way she made us feel. Natural and unnatural at the same time.

The A side of Grace Jones's first album, *Portfolio*, released by Island Records in 1977, is composed of an eighteen-and-a-half-minute-long disco medley of covers from the Broadway musicals *A Little Night Music*, *A Chorus Line*, and *Annie*. She sends in the clowns and tells us what she did for love and assures us that the sun will come out tomorrow. The results are, at least to me, mostly forgettable. But then I turn the record over. Jones launches the other side of the album with what has become one of her signature hits: a seven-and-a-half-minute-long cover of French diva Edith Piaf's classic 1947 torch song, "La vie en rose." In the original, Piaf's alto voice trembles with hope ("Life in Rosy Hues") embroidered along its edges with the dark threads of sorrow. It's a song of and for its time, capturing the sentiments of devastation and deliverance among those who survived World War II. Jones transforms the song into a bossa nova–styled disco groove rippling with notes stretched languorously enough to wind down the dancers in the early morning hours at the club. After its release, Jones's cover was, in fact, in frequent rotation among nightclub DJs as closing time crept in.

Jones's version opens with an instrumental prelude, the synthesizer and a strummed guitar inviting us to wade leisurely into the song. Nearly two whole minutes with no vocals. Instead, we're bobbing along the gentle waves of the music. For Jones, ever the disco diva, the only way to glimpse a life in rosy hues is to move and move and move your body and, ideally, to move it closer to and in undulating rhythm with other bodies. When her voice finally arrives at minute 1:49, she *mmmmmmmsssss* and *aaaaahhhhhhhhs* before landing softly into the lyrics at minute 2:20. We can't help but surrender as she pulls us in deeper and deeper. Her voice is a siren's lull that turns to a snarling growl for eight unfurling seconds on the word "vie" at 4:30 minutes in and then turns back from riptide to soothing ripple until the closing propulsive minute of the song when she repeats the lyric, "La vie en rose," a total of eight times. Jones makes of that insistent line an incantation, a Prospero-command willing our bodies to move and keep moving until our cheeks are flushed with rosy hues. Jones's "Life in Pink" is tinged with the smear of blood on its cheek.

One of my favorite memories of dancing until my cheeks flushed red was at the Aragon Ballroom in Chicago at the Celia Cruz concert during the spring of 1995. She took to the stage—at last—at 1 a.m. and she called out to us—*¡Azúcar!*— and I swooned and my legs wobbled and then caught their quick-quick-slow stride like a newborn colt. I don't remember her set list or even what pair of her famous gravity-defying platform shoes she wore that night. But I do remember my outfit: a vintage maillot swimsuit the color of a canary topped off with a silk sash tied at the waist. And leather-soled shoes meant for dancing all night. The diva inspires our fashion risks, teaching us how to style ourselves for the life we long for and not just the one we're currently living. Her own style is both inimitable and reverently or campily quoted.

Dolly Parton's platinum wigs and rhinestone-gilded cinched waist. Grace Jones's closely cropped, geometric hair and Afro-futurist-armored outfits.

Divas know how to accessorize. They are known by how they wear or wield their accessories: Aretha Franklin walks onstage at the Kennedy Center and tosses her clutch on the piano, lets her fur fall to the floor. Divas know that everything within or even out of reach is a potential prop meant for handling, for possession. They know all about how to inhabit a costume. For her video "Perfect," Grace Jones commissioned Keith Haring to design a sixty-foot-wide skirt underneath which was a lift built for her inevitable ascension. And when she rose, she took the entire floor with her, her skirt swallowing up all who worshipped her and all who did not.

The diva is often rendered by and through synecdoche: *The Queen's Throat*, *The Diva's Mouth*, the gardenia in her hair. A signature gesture or song or slogan or body part is what makes her and what makes her known: Tina's shoulder shrugs or her legs that go all the way up to her throat or Celia's custom-made shoes or her shout—*¡Azúcar!*—evoking at once the workings of desire and a history of enslaved labor. *We have the deep throats*, Lauren Bacall once said to Grace Jones. We know the diva synecdochally. And from her parts we assemble our lives and our outfits. In her parts, we are made whole.

I danced to Celia Cruz at the Aragon the same spring that the pop diva Selena was murdered two weeks shy of her twenty-fourth birthday. We were the same age, both Tejanas who grew up speaking Spanglish, cultivating a working-class brown femme style, and perfecting our dance moves to cumbias and Janet Jackson songs. Fans everywhere assembled to mourn her passing, to mourn in her passing so many losses that marked our brown lives. It was my first year of graduate school, and I embarked on my studies in the shadow of Selena's death. I didn't yet know I would one day write a book about the ways we grieve Selena in an effort to assemble ourselves, to make ourselves whole again. All I knew then was that a diva had died. It happened one day when I least expected it.

You could say that the diva, as we once knew her, also died in the 1990s. Or, like the mythic, fluttering creature at the end of *Godzilla v. Mothra*, the diva met her demise only to be reborn in the proliferation of diva-spawn: pop music diva, domestic diva, tween diva. Some would say that the diva was democratized; others would argue that she was diminished to an ailing noun propped on the crutch of an adjective: fashion diva, Disney diva, tennis diva. Many would agree that the widespread popularization of diva worship signaled yet another instance of appropriation and commodification of queer cultural practices and styles. Suddenly, it seemed, divas were everywhere—no longer just my own obsession—and the public loved them and loathed them and wanted to be them and wanted them gone. *These days, you can't throw the Hope Diamond without hitting a diva*, Andrew Essex despaired in a 1998 cover story for *Entertainment Weekly*. By the end of the 1990s, VH1 had summoned popular music divas like Mariah Carey and Celine Dion to "Save the Music" in public schools, Virginia Slims had sponsored the "Dueling Divas" concert that would crown a local-area all-female band as reigning divas to benefit the Tampa AIDS Network, Faye Dunaway had portrayed Maria Callas in the touring production of Terrence McNally's Tony Award-winning *Master Class*, and "diva" had become just another brand and an increasingly dirty word.

The diva was born. The diva was reborn. Over the last fifty years, the diva has gone from disco to discourse. Diva discourse has come to signal more than simply a way of talking about strong, complicated women with strong, complicated voices. Diva discourse, it now seems, expresses a simultaneous repudiation and embrace of feminism—that is a postfeminist view—in which strong, complicated women can only be (dis)regarded as divas. Hence the popular saying, "She's such a diva!" delivered with equal parts derision and envy. Diva discourse has emerged as a powerful public forum in which we proclaim or decry our place as communities of color or conditioned consumers, as growing girls or gay grooms, as twenty-first-century mothers or all the single ladies. Diva discourse signals the commodification and containment of the diva's threat and also expresses our anxieties about it. *I hate that word diva*, Grace Jones declares. *It's been so abused! Every singer given a makeover or a few weeks on a talent show seems to be called a diva these days! Christ Almighty. Where's the exclusivity? It's so commercial now. Call me something else.*

My daughter was born the same year I published my book about Selena's afterlife. As a new author of a book about a diva and a new mother to a baby girl, I couldn't help but take note of the ways I was accosted by the burgeoning market of "diva girl" products: frilly curtains with the word "diva" in looping pink script, "Diva Girl" onesies and diva girl manicures-with-mommy at the local salon. The Barbie Diva Collection had launched in 2001, the Cast Album for the 2003 Broadway musical *Wicked* went platinum by 2006, and Disney had begun creating original television shows featuring tween girls with supernatural or diva powers. "Diva" no longer seemed to describe or decry accomplished women of a certain age but to condition girls or would-be girls of any age to be hyper-feminine consumers.

My daughter was born the month after a 2009 *Newsweek* article fretted, "Are We Turning Tweens into 'Generation Diva'?" That same year Disney released *Hannah Montana: The Movie*, based on the wildly popular tween television series in which Miley Cyrus plays a character named Miley Stewart who's an ordinary girl by day, but who, by night, lives a secret life as Hannah Montana, a singing diva sensation. Oh, and her god(diva-)mother happens to be Dolly Parton. On the show and in "real life." A tween diva playing a girl playing a tween diva watched over by a diva godmother playing a diva godmother on TV.

Is this what the diva has come down to? A diva is a girl and a girl is a girl aspiring to be a diva, adorned with sparkly merchandise and hailed to perform in the singular spotlight. Diva as a mode of disciplining twenty-first-century girls into neoliberal models of individualism and consumption. Diva as a means of convincing girls that singing along to a power ballad in a sequined t-shirt emblazoned with "Li'l Diva" equals actual power. Or diva as a way girls sing out against these forces. A girl playing at diva to hear the sound of her own voice.

What did diva even mean anymore? And why was I—a longtime diva devotee—so unsettled by such diva proliferation and transformation? With the help of Google Ngram, launched in 2010 as my daughter was learning to walk, I decided to track the usage of the word "diva" over time and discovered a dramatic rise—a near 400 percent increase!—in the appearance of the term since the early 1990s. What were we talking about when we talked, with ever increasing fervor and frequency, about divas? Guided by my unflagging devotion to divas, my scholarly interest in female performers, and my motherly concern for my daughter's future as part of "Generation Diva," I did what any college professor does when she wants to learn the answers to questions that puzzle her. I taught a class about it.

I taught my first seminar on divas in the fall of 2009 and have taught the course nearly every year since then. After more than a decade spent in the classroom with students— brilliant young women and incisive trans and nonbinary folx and fabulous gay boys from the "Millennial Generation" and "Generation Z" who had grown up watching all those Disney tween shows or had encountered the history of Harlem drag balls in *RuPaul's Drag Race* and *Pose* or were devoted members of Lady Gaga's "Little Monsters" or Beyonce's "Beyhive"—I learned that I wasn't alone. My enduring diva devotion wasn't just some form of Generation X, previous-wave feminist, musical-loving nostalgia (though, truth be told, I'm not above that). Year after year, students from across class backgrounds and college majors and hometowns and sexual orientations and racial and gender identifications enrolled to study, with utmost seriousness and delight, all about divas and their roles in our lives. Over the years, I've noticed that we've talked about divas as a way of talking about difference and artistry and belonging and power and style and race and girlhood and discipline and pleasure and feminism and grief and family and possibility and gender and fantasy and survival and capitalism and sexuality and freedom, and, above all, as a way of talking, with utmost seriousness and delight, about our own lives.

My daughter was born between the opening of *Wicked* in 2003 and the release of *Frozen* in 2013. Between Idina Menzel belting "Defying Gravity" and Idina Menzel belting "Let It Go." By my daughter's fifth birthday, we were living in Paris for a semester while I was on a teaching exchange, coming to terms with our shitty French and stumbling along streets still marked by the presence of divas: Sarah Bernhardt's flower-strewn tomb at Cimetière du Père Lachaise, Place Josephine Baker, Place Edith Piaf, bars where Nina Simone once sang, nightclubs where Grace Jones once danced. Yet, for all of my aspirations to retrace their steps, my only diva souvenir from Paris is a video of my daughter singing—a cappella and with emotive hand gestures—"Let It Go." By early 2014 all the Parisian girls were letting it go. My daughter sang and sang and sang that diva anthem just like countless other girls at her public *maternelle*. Yes, even in Paris—French anti-American posturing be damned—*Let it go, les petites filles ont chanté, Let it go!*

My daughter was born. And she is reborn with every diva song she's hailed to sing. Which makes her "Generation Diva,"

"Let It Go"

I suppose. Which makes me want to make sense of what the diva has become in the generation between her birth and mine. Which makes me want to reach my voice, inspired by the divas I've loved, across a range of registers—ode and elegy, memoir and manifesto, love letter and critical commentary, longing whisper and audacious belt—as an homage to all the ways divas are born and reborn. Because divas endure. Because even as the term "diva" circulates as a misogynist label for women who dare to insist upon themselves, Beyoncé is hailed as a leading force for Black feminist and economic power and Dolly Parton is lauded for saving our forsaken country through her million-dollar donation to COVID-19 vaccine research. Because my aging Tías still rouge their cheeks and show up at all the Mexican weddings to dance circles around the rest of us. Because Grace Jones, at age 75, continues to hula hoop in a leotard and body paint onstage in front of her legions of adoring fans. Because a diva never retires. As Jones reminds us: *When I retire, I'm dead, and even then, I will be reincarnated. I will remain on the move. Even death won't stop me. It never has.*

2

Diva Style

Tía Lucia, Prima Prima Donna

Lucia was my first. Tía Lucia Virginia Martinez Bustillo.
Sometimes Lucy or Lucille. To a few: *Tía Chia*. The accent
over the "i" in Lucia dropped somewhere along the way like
when a diva drops her fur on the stage. My grandmother's sister
so technically my great-aunt, but she was simply Tía to everyone who knew her. Seems like all the folks of color I know have
one. That influential Tía or Auntie who dwells on the margins
of the family, of propriety even, and who models an adamantly
singular and deliciously adorned life. Grace Jones speaks of
the *delightful naughtiness* of her Aunt Sybil who showed her *how
you could put on makeup without it causing a catastrophe*. Wesley
Morris muses, *My appreciation of what an Auntie is: she does her,
she's living her life, she spreads joy and love and not bitterness, she's
a little grandiose, a little self-absorbed, but maybe wise and a little mystical and silly and coolly clueless, and maybe she's drunk, but
that's OK*. Auntie-divas or proto–prima donnas who taught us
to step out in style or to step out of line, who took our hand
and guided it as we held the eyeliner. Tías who assured us that

everything was going to be all right—or not—and who helped us craft our own sense of style as armor against the inevitable assaults. Tías who taught us how to cantilever ourselves across catastrophe, who introduced us to opera or, in my case, oysters. Tías who taught us not to fear the flesh. Who made an art out of accessorizing it.

Tía Lucia taught me how to fashion not just my body but my life. For a diva like Tía Lucia, the most important act of creation was self-creation. She sent me hundreds of letters over the years. In each one, she narrates daily life with the keen understanding that she is in the starring role. Such flair and conviction and delight that she's nobody's co-star. Self-aggrandizement isn't necessary for the diva because she already knows the self *is* grand. She's just telling it like it is. *Well, guess who this is? Your "Favorite Aunt,"* she would, on occasion, launch her letters to me.

On the front of the envelope of the letters she sent, in the space between her return address and mine, Tía would sometimes write, *Greatest Writer* or *The Famous Writer*. I never knew if she was referring to me or to herself.

Tía Lucia couldn't carry a tune or dance en pointe but she could carry something off. Cat-eye sunglasses. Clip-on earrings the size of saucers. A Christmas sweater—unironically. Someone else's money. Style was for her not simply an expression of self-possession but of self-preservation. What else to do but fashion the self in a force field of glamour when life (and men) lash out with regular assaults? For the diva, style is where she turns when it comes down to "by any means necessary." Tía Lucia refused marriage proposals and nursed black eyes from more than one lover and threw raw eggs at her sister-in-law's house and rode the bus to Vegas and back—all while keeping her black wool coat buttoned and unsullied. The same coat she wore in 1981 when she buttoned me up in my best coat and drove us downtown for the opening of the new Hyatt

Regency with its glass elevators overlooking the sparkling lights of the riverwalk that snaked through downtown crowded with rich gringo tourists. She showed me how to walk in like we belonged there, pretending we were hotel patrons so we could ride those elevators, rising and falling and rising again and again, looking out for once instead of in, all night long.

Divas teach us how to style our lives in the service of adventure and pleasure. In her song "Red Shoes," Dolly Parton fondly remembers how playing dress-up in her Aunt Lucy's red shoes trained her to stride through the far-flung adventures and the daily grind of her life in a pair of her own red shoes. My Aunt Lucy turned the everyday into a holiday. She said to me once, in all seriousness, *You know, I was thinking of hiring an orchestra and opening up my cedar chest.* Every moment styled into an occasion for ceremony and celebration. *I'll close for now. I have to take a shower, wash my hair, and get ready to "Rumble"*—Party, Party, Party, Party.

The diva's resourcefulness is unparalleled. Indeed, it was for Tía and working-class divas like her the source of her

Tissue box postcard

greatest artistry. She wrote her letters to me over the years on whatever was at hand, and when her embossed stationery or five-and-dime notebook paper ran out, she'd cut up the cardboard tissue boxes around her apartment and transform them into elegant postcards.

The diva is an alchemical force capable of turning anything she touches into an object of beauty. *Life is too short to be ugly*, she once declared in òne of her letters.

Tía opened up her cedar chest and her closet to me. I spent many of my teenaged days encased in her empire-waist dresses from the '50s or her white leather Nehru jacket from the '60s. It was the '80s—all Bill Blass shoulder pads and Reaganomics—and I was desperate for another pattern by which to measure my life. I aspired to fill in her silhouette. The diva beckons us to become her, blurring the boundaries between identification and desire. We want her. We want to be her. She fills us with want. What I wanted was the powder-blue scarf Tía brought back from her trip to London in 1964. Nothing particularly fancy: poly-blend, pure kitsch, tourist prints of Big Ben and Buckingham Palace. But for me it was a talisman to ward off the ordinary. More than souvenir: a promise of elsewhere. The first time I folded the square cloth into a triangle and tied it

Lucia in London

around my neck I was a seventh grader in a secondhand Jordache coat, all glasses and crooked teeth and boobs I'd yet to grow into. But the scarf. The ceremony of folding and draping and fastening. The practiced élan. I was transformed. I don't think I took that scarf off until college and even then only to replace it with one secured from my own elsewhere adventures.

Not long after she retired from her secretarial job of 40 years, Tía Lucia moved into the Granada Homes, an affordable senior-living high-rise that was initially built in the 1920s as the Plaza Hotel and still boasted a ballroom on the top floor. A diva deserves no less. I held my wedding reception in that ballroom. Before the dance, I made a dramatic costume change, having commissioned one of my costume-design students to make me a red flamenco dress. Sometime between the mariachis and the DJ spinning songs by Al Green and Celia Cruz, Tía slipped away downstairs to her apartment for her own costume change. She reemerged, making her entrance in a red blouse and sparkling jewelry that matched—outdid—my dress. We danced together until dawn.

One of my most prized diva accessories—my saint's relic—is one of Tía's charm bracelets, a costume piece she picked up in Vegas sometime in the '70s. One of the charms is an open-faced rectangular box that holds—and when unclasped, releases—two miniature dice. Sometimes I roll them. Most times it's enough just to know I can.

Tía, like all divas, was always game for life. Never afraid of the big gamble. At ease with winning big and undeterred by big losses. Her letters regularly chronicled in detail her wins and losses. *$50 on the Horse Races—A new Jackpot every hour on the hour—I slapped down some green—Won six times last night.* She styled herself to be unconstrained by the hard realities of life. She would regularly make her own reality, guided as she was by the rules of chance and dreams and fantasy and all that

Lucky charms

is fabulous. But her way was not simply frivolous. Above all, she refused to concede dignity amidst life's onslaught of indignities. *I sure won a lot. I'll be able to put in my phone again real soon.*

Not long after her phone got reinstalled, Tía called to tell me she had lost her car. I failed, at first, to understand fully what had happened.

> *Where did you last park it?*
>
> > *No, Debbie. I lost it to the slots.*

A diva like Tía risks it all, and she does it all out in public. The spectacle of her suffering is evidence of her perseverance. And, sometimes, those of us who love her most bear the costs of her risky business. Once, Tía offered to help me sell a box of candy bars for my drama club costume fundraiser. I never saw the candy or the cash again. She carried off with it—and then carried on as usual. The diva is unrepentant. Sometimes

Lucia and her car

she leaves you in a bind. Or in debt. Or in a state of awe that is equal parts rapture and resentment. And why shouldn't she when caprice is her craft? A diva like Tía teaches us how to love women who are simultaneously grand and imperfect, how to hold admiration and indignation, how to insist on your gloriously messy brown self when the world never will. She throws eggs and rides the bus when the car's been repossessed and she does it in an impeccably brooched and buttoned black wool coat. Her signature style as easy and alarming as taking candy from a baby.

Candy and a baby, Easter Sunday, 1972

3

———————

Diva Movidas
Rita and Anita

There's a photo of Tía Lucia and my mother from one of their downtown weekend excursions circa 1955 taken by Orvil G. Mosher, one of the regularly stationed sidewalk photographers who hawked their services along Houston Street in downtown San Antonio. In the shot, Tía is dressed in a wool gabardine calf-length skirt and a perfectly pressed white blouse buttoned all the way up to its Peter Pan collar, her mouth stretched in mid-command. My mother, a ribbon tied into a bow atop her head and Mary Janes buckled over her ankle-socked feet, peers directly and purposefully into the camera's lens. Perhaps they've just walked out of Joske's Department Store with its extravagant "Fantasyland" Christmas display sprawled across the entire fourth floor, their arms weighed down with packages and their sloughed-off coats. Perhaps they are on their way to the Majestic or the Alameda, the grand movie houses they frequented in those years.

At the Majestic they would drape their sweaters over their

Lucia and Connie shopping on Houston Street

shoulders in the air-conditioned dark and catch the latest Hollywood movie musicals—*always something with dancing* is what my mother remembers—Leslie Caron and Gene Kelly twirling together along the Seine in *An American in Paris* or Cyd Charisse leaping from her bed to perform a pas de deux with successive parts of her discarded wardrobe in *Silk Stockings*. Inside the Alameda, the dimming lights would ignite the glow of the black-light murals that lined the walls and depicted scenes from the histories of Texas on one side and Mexico on the other. Within this milieu, Tía and my mother would delight in the golden era of classic Mexican films—the high melodrama of the diva-as-*soldadera* battle between Maria Félix and Dolores del Río in *La Cucaracha* (released in English as *The Soldiers of Pancho Villa*)—and live Spanish-language musical acts playing accordion-driven conjuntos or singing diva-throated boleros.

They would pass the weekends in this way, shuffling in a practiced choreography across the borders of these worlds shimmering with Fantasyland tinsel and film flicker and synchronized pirouettes and phosphorescent paint. All of it training my mother's spectatorial sensibilities, piquing her submerged longings, shaping her code-switching voice. *Ay, I wish I'd become a dancer*, she will sigh to me more than half a century later.

My mother doesn't remember her first encounter with *West Side Story*. All she knows is she's always loved it. What she does remember are the countless afternoons she spent sprawled across her bed singing along to songs from the show and other popular hits on the radio that she received as a present in grade school—not long after the stage musical premiered on Broadway in 1957. The same year that my father immigrated with his family from Mexico and landed several neighborhoods over. By 1962, when the musical's cast album reached Number 5 on *Billboard*'s Pop Album chart, my mom had already been crooning and leaping from her bed to dance along to her growing collection of 45s on the record player she had begged for and secured the year before on her twelfth birthday.

Her memory falters when she tries to recall the first time she saw the 1961 film version of *West Side Story* but is fairly certain it was when NBC aired it for its television premiere over the course of two successive nights in March 1972. At the time, she and I were sharing a bed in the front room of my grandparents' house. It was the same year my father would return from Vietnam. I don't remember the details; I was only just learning to walk. But over those two spring nights, just as I had many times before and would many times after, I was no doubt nestled beside her, drifting off to the snapping sounds of the opening number.

Like my mother, I can't recall the first time I began learning the lyrics and the choreography to *West Side Story*. In my memory, I am seven or eight. The amber glow from the television set is the only illumination in the shuttered room. I am in bed with my mother, our bodies curled together in the shape of a single question mark, my arm resting along her belly's soft folds, legs nestled against the stubble of her calves. The sheets are musky and worn thin. We are singing, our breaths spilling into each other's as our harmonies falter. We know every line, every lyric. We scoff at the brown-cake makeup. Roll our eyes at the accents. We believe that, yes, a boy like that *could* kill your brother. We cry when Bernardo dies. We curse. We croon. We curse. And we return and return and return to it— at first, as a Saturday night network feature, and in later years as a Sunday afternoon cable channel offering or an overdue VHS rental or a scratched DVD on a Tuesday morning. We can't get enough. We hold our breaths when Anita's petticoat flares, her leg kicked up and stretching to forever, to the smattering of stars above, to some beyond somewhere far from here.

In the decades since its opening night, *West Side Story* has been *the* story brown folks like my mom and I have had to reckon with. Many of us have catalogued and condemned the musical's depictions of criminal "Latin" youth and overly sexual "Latin" women all adorned with an abundant application of brownface makeup. *Why do we all have to be the same color?* Rita Moreno will later recall thinking during the filming, *It was like going to war. If you wanted to be in that movie, you had to lather on the war paint.*

And yet, the musical also endures as a paradoxical and often pleasurable cultural text by which many of us, or at least those of us over 50, have come to know ourselves and each other. Over the last half century, many of us have turned to the musical as the point of entry or departure for our own art or crit-

Rita stretching to forever

icism or stories of self-knowing—from the tear-jerking 2007 finale of *Ugly Betty*'s first season to the fire escape–strewn stage design of Lin-Manuel Miranda's 2008 musical *In the Heights*, from the critical writings of scholar Alberto Sandoval-Sanchez and filmmaker Frances Negrón-Muntaner to the recollections shared by Supreme Court Justice Sonia Sotomayor and jazz percussionist Bobby Sanabria, from Selena's 1995 dance club version of "A Boy Like That" to Jennifer Lopez's 2009 interview and photo spread in *Vanity Fair*, in which she recalled watching *West Side Story* 37 times during her childhood in the Bronx: *I never wanted to be that wimpy Maria who sits around pining for her guy. I wanted to be Anita, who danced her way to the top.*

West Side Story, which premiered on Broadway in 1957, is generally classified as a golden-age musical play. Historically framed by *Oklahoma* (1943) and *Fiddler on the Roof* (1964), golden-age musicals are characterized by their attempts to integrate and unify their various structural elements (score, lyrics, book, choreography) into one cohesive and total work. In this way, golden-age musicals depart from the musical comedies that preceded them by having the score follow the book (not the other way around), that is, by using songs to further the plot or express a character's inner psychology rather than featuring songs that serve simply as star vehicles or as easily excerpted radio standards. Since the songs in golden-age musicals propel the plot and character development, the characters who sing the most often are the ones who are positioned to elicit the most audience sympathy.

West Side Story follows the golden-age model with its use of songs as the means through which characters and subplots from different locations converge ("Tonight"), through its drive for unification, embodied in the romantic pairing of Maria and Tony, and through its depiction of the bonds established within racially marked and gendered worlds. Both the stage version of the musical and its film adaptation, directed by Robert Wise and Jerome Robbins, share Leonard Bernstein's music, Stephen Sondheim's lyrics, and Robbins's choreography, which draws its inspiration from ballet and social dance forms of the period.

But *West Side Story* is known mostly for the ways it departs from the conventions of other golden-age musicals. As an adaptation of *Romeo and Juliet*, it ends tragically and therefore without the characteristic upbeat, ensemble-driven finale. More than anything, what sets *West Side Story* apart from the other musicals of its time is that it tells its story primarily through dance. In fact, Jerome Robbins is the first choreographer credited with "authorizing" a musical. In the world of this play, choreography is the prevailing meaning maker; movement and not just song expresses character, affiliation, struggle, and desire. Indeed, the first sung song doesn't appear in the film for twenty minutes; instead, stylized movements, such as the famous crouching-and-snapping phrase, introduce us to the Sharks and the Jets. Within this context, the character who *dances* the most—and the best—garners the most sympathy. It's no wonder then that we so often identify with Anita: the formal logic of the musical and the particular demands of the role insist that we root for her—the character in the best dress executing the best dance moves.

And Anita *moves*. She moves across dance styles and harmonies and perspectives and the borderlines of turf and tribe. She moves more impressively and more expansively and more unpredictably than any other character in a musical that values and makes its meanings from movement above all. By which I mean, she moves like a diva. *West Side Story* may be an ensemble musical preoccupied with group belonging, but it's still a musical, which means there's likely a diva within it delightedly pulling at the threads of the story it weaves. No surprise, then, that Chita Rivera gained acclaim as Anita in 1957 and that Rita Moreno secured a Best Supporting Actress Oscar for her portrayal in the 1961 film. No surprise, then, that when my mother and I watch and rewatch, we are enthralled by both Rita and Anita, by Rita-as-Anita, by the diva and—as—her role. Simultaneously singular and plural.

My mother was raised in a neighborhood that was 100 percent brown, or, more specifically, Mexican—as she and her kin would call themselves then. But she attended schools that were populated largely by white ethnic kids—mostly German- and Polish-descended—who lived in the surrounding neighborhoods. At the time, Mexicans were legally categorized as "white" even though the legacy of land dispossession following the end of the Mexican-American War and the enduring practices of discrimination—"No Dogs or Mexicans" posted in restaurant and storefront windows throughout the city—prevented them from benefitting much from the operations of white supremacy. But it did mean that my mother and the other kids on her block went to the same schools as the white kids, which is not to say that they received the same education nor that they experienced anything resembling equality. All my mother remembers about grade-school social studies is the frequent suspensions the teacher would issue to her and her brothers and cousins for speaking Spanish. She saw and heard and mostly followed the rules set by white folks at school, but her social world beyond it was 100 percent Mexican. My mother recalls as her only interaction with a white kid during the early years of her schooling the time a gringo boy taunted her by calling her chubby. Hers was a world strictly ordered by turf and tribe, by the dividing line that separated her Mexican neighborhood from the rest.

In fact, my mother's most vivid memory from her elementary school days was the time the teachers taught the children German and Polish folk dances—countless rehearsals that strove to discipline her body into those stiff-spined, clacking rhythms. There were no Mexican folk dances in the curriculum despite the school's split demographics. Instead, the teachers insisted that my mother and her cousin, Rudy Jr., perform the "Mexican Hat Dance"—that paragon of brown-face, gringo fantasy—as a featured entertainment at the school assembly. Apparently, this was considered an honor.

My mother obliged even as she understood the sham. And my grandmother even bought a Mexican folk skirt hand-painted with a bucolic Sonoran desert scene and spent the evenings sewing sequins along its voluminous border. It was a performance after all, and her girl had to showcase some semblance of, if not authenticity, then at least self-preservation. My mother doesn't remember any of the steps she was forced to learn, but she can still feel how the skirt encircled her like a force field.

Over the years it became a family heirloom, handed down to me and then to each of my younger girl cousins—with every new recipient, more sequins generously applied—and finally to my daughter, all of us taking part in a long tradition of enacting joyous brown girl pleasure, twirling across the stage or the yard, the kitchen or the parade route, as the skirt rose and waved at our waists: an iridescent wingspan made for liftoff.

Sprawling wingspan

When my daughter grew out of it, I mounted the skirt and hung it over our hearth—a sparkling homage to the family lineage of divas-in-training learning to perform beyond the constraints of the folk-fantasy roles often assigned to us as brown girls growing up in America.

In *West Side Story*, Anita wears a dress that also encircles her like a force field. Her skirt extends the expansive reach of her dancing body, every part of her rippling widely across so much space. The full skirt is buoyed by petticoat ruffles, its voluminous crinoline plumes unfurled into an iridescent wingspan made for liftoff. At the dance in the gymnasium, the Sharks and the Jets enact their turf war through dueling mambos. But all I ever remember from the scene is Anita

Mexican folk dress-up

Connie takes the crown

and the broad, sinuous sweeps of her legs and arms, the wide undulations of her purple-tulled skirt, the flash of her hoop earrings as she flings her head back. All the space she takes. All the abandon and all the control. She keeps step with the spiraling frenzy of the mambo's tempo, riding its surges until she threads the eye of its storm with such precision, with such élan, with the steadied reach of her outstretched leg. She spins and shakes and stomps and shifts and shifts and shifts her weight and then—suddenly—she stills, a lightning flash, and reaches high to take Bernardo's raised hand as she slides like a note down the scale into a lunge and as soon as she touches down—a lightning strike—she drags her toe along the floor—

the ease, the extension, the suspension of time—until she is fully upright and kicking again, her body the thunderbolt and the god who throws it. She returns to her risen stance. And keeps on dancing.

In her final year of junior high in 1964, my mother was crowned Queen at the spring dance. *Maybe it was Princess*, she later recalls, *They said someone cheated—like maybe a teacher had rigged the voting—but I didn't care. They gave me the crown. And I took it.*

After the dance in the gym, Anita ascends the stairs to the rooftop along with the other Sharks. She's fighting with Bernardo about "life in *América*." Exasperated, Bernardo turns to his fellow Sharks, proclaiming, *Look! Instead of a shampoo, she's been brainwashed! She's given up Puerto Rico and now she's queer for Uncle Sam.* While Anita responds coyly, *Oh, no! That's not true*, she immediately launches into singing, "America," mocking the men's nostalgic devotion to Puerto Rico while executing flawless Caribbean-inflected dance moves. While Bernardo means that Anita's sweet on Uncle Sam—foolishly seduced into the imperial arms of the USA—I think he's onto something more. She *is* queer for Uncle Sam. Despite the lyrics, there's nothing straightforward about Anita's relationship to "America." Rita's movements as Anita provoke and point to the pleasures and risks for so many of us brown folks, not of belonging, but of longing. A longing for a place somewhere beyond the here and now, beyond the historically drawn borders of "America." Anita may sing of assimilation, but she dances its undoing.

Just watch what she does with the paso doble.

The choreography for "America" relies heavily on the erect extensions of the spine in both ballet and the paso doble, an "International Latin" ballroom form danced primarily in competitive rather than social settings. The paso doble stages the stylized march of a Spanish bullfight (at least, as it was imagined by the French who invented the dance). The male lead typically portrays the matador while the female partner and her flowing dress represent his cape or occasionally the bull to be tamed. Traditionally, the paso doble departs from other ballroom dances by featuring the male rather than the female partner: the high chest, elongated vertical posture, and aggressive gestures of the male typically tower over and provide the frame that contains the more flowing movements of his female partner.

That is, until Anita dances in *West Side Story*, purple petticoat flaring.

She sings in unison with her fellow Shark women hailing the possibilities of belonging in "América," but she moves distinctively, singularly. When Bernardo and two other Shark men launch into their sharp, swift, paso doble–inspired steps, Anita breaks from the herd and charges at them with high kicks and sweeping arms. Alone, she takes on all three men, shaking the skirt of her dress toward them, chasing them to the outermost edges of the frame. She's reversed the traditional roles of the dance: no longer just the cape, she becomes the bullfighter who wields it.

The high kick, the arched back, she makes of her body a stampede. Anita keeps breaking into a dance solo in an ensemble song-and-dance number all about national belonging. She moves in her own expansive sphere while remaining in step with the Sharks to whom she claims loyalty. She's simultaneously a part of the group and apart from it. She moves through "America" with a sense of *ni de aquí, ni de allá* [neither of here, nor of there] that so many of us brown folks feel in relation to national belonging. The way we inhabit and make spectacular those darkened spaces like the movie theatres of my mother's youth with phosphorescent painted scenes of the histories from each opposing side. Her

dancing calls to mind the way brown folks approach "Uncle
Sam," the way we claim our *right to be different and to belong*,
as scholar Renato Rosaldo writes. Difference and belonging,
difference-in-belonging.

Keep watching. Now watch it again.

The high kick, the arched back, the stalking, the circling,
the pounce. Rita's mastery of the notoriously exacting rig-
ors of Jerome Robbins's choreography and the undisciplined
delight in her body's movement beyond it. She doesn't just
nail the steps, she builds her own inviolable space beyond the
white-fantasies-of-brown-movement imagined by Robbins
and the other white male creators of the show. There is in
Rita's mauve-blurred movements as Anita both a sense of well-
rehearsed control and improvisatory curve, a sense of what my
mother would call *movidas*, of finding a way when there seems
to be no way, of creating space where none is ceded. *Movidas*
are not just ways of making do but making do with brown flair,
of hustling so smoothly it looks like dancing.

Rita moves with precision and capaciousness and unre-
strained flamboyance in all directions, spinning out and
rotating on her own axis. Anita may be linked romantically
to Bernardo in the script, but Rita-as-Anita moves in ways
that are conspicuously, spectacularly singular. She refuses
to move in a straight line—and why should she when the
playing field is so full of obstacles? All brown folks know
there's no straight-forward path toward securing our place
here, only the well-rehearsed control and improvisatory
curve and sartorial flair and audacious joy we perform in
our movidas. We recognize in Anita—in Rita's diva turn as
Anita—our own refusals to follow a linear or straight(-for-
ward) progression toward assimilation and its demands for
"monogamous" national affiliation. She makes us feel queer
for Uncle Sam.

Anita charging

My mother wanted to learn the steps. Throughout high school and for years after it, my mother spent nearly every Saturday tuning in to *American Bandstand* and *Soul Train*, learning and practicing the latest dance moves. She rehearsed them all—the shifting weight and opposing pull of the Twist and the plunging stomp of the Pony—and also the ones done at family weddings—the galloping beat of the cumbia and the dizzying spin of the Mexican polka—in an effort to work out and move through all that couldn't be worked out or moved through in the choreography of her daily life. She danced at home every Saturday—moving alone in steps made to be performed with others—like a Tejana version of *Hairspray's* Tracy Turnblad dreaming and dancing toward an elsewhere. She was dancing by herself in my grandparents' living room, perfecting her moves so well that one boyfriend broke up with her because he refused to believe she had learned the moves on her own, convinced instead that she was going around with other guys to practice. A boy like that.

There is something so brown in the way Anita moves—and not just because she can dance the mambo or the paso doble or because it's the only role in the musical's long production history that's often cast with an actual Latina diva. Indeed, Anita—from Chita Rivera and Karen Olivo on Broadway to Rita Moreno and Ariana DeBose in film, from Santana Lopez's casting as Anita in an episode arc in *Glee* to J Lo's reenactment of Anita's scenes from the film in her *Vanity Fair* photo spread—has historically been an "authenticating" role for Latina actresses. But that's not it. What feels so brown about the way Anita moves is the way she moves in relation to others: at once distinct from and simultaneously synchronized to the rhythms of those with whom she seeks community. A sense of *being singular plural* that scholar José E. Muñoz once described as a key—and queer—feature of *feeling brown*.

I want to reach out to José and ask him if this is what he meant by *feeling brown*, but like other boys whom my mother and I once knew, he is gone.

Still, I ask him. Because I'm 100 percent Mexican and we are accustomed to talking to the dead.

José, I say across the divide, *If you're brown, really feeling brown, clearing enough space with your kicked-up legs and your unfurled skirt to create what you once called a brown commons, if you're brown like that, are you queer? If you're queer for Uncle Sam are you brown? Does Anita feel brown to you?*

He is standing against the wall on the other side, his voice carrying across the space between us, cautioning me not to get too carried away, not to overuse or misapply my words, not to empty *queer* or *brown* of their specificity, of their specific potency. He keeps speaking but I'm having trouble hearing

him because where he is the music is pounding and there are
so many brown bodies filling the dance floor between us.

He speaks into the pulsing crowd. *A brown commons . . . is
an example of a collectivity with and through the incommensurable*,
his voice absorbed now by all the bodies pulsing together and
pulling apart. Here it's "Latin" night every night—*Brown, it is
important to mention, is not strictly the shared experience of harm
between people*—everyone getting down and feeling brown to
the sounds of Selena's club remix of "A Boy Like That"—*it is
also the potential for the refusal and resistance to that often-systemic
harm*—all of us pulsing to the irregular rhythms of the brown
commons, the common brownness, made by our movements.

To be brown is to dance with the dead. To be brown is to
move. Brownness is migratory. Which means it's subject to
surveillance. Brownness can elude the black-and-white vision
of the surveilling eyes. Which means that brown bodies can
sometimes move in ways Black bodies aren't allowed to move.
Brownness can sometimes pass because of the ways it has
been used to pronounce its non-Blackness or anti-Blackness.
Brownness can be slippery in its movement, for sure. But, to
be brown is also to refuse the documented terms of citizenship
or racial categorization established by the nation. That is, to
be brown is to be *queer for Uncle Sam*. Brownness refuses to be
still for the state. Brownness refuses to pledge allegiance to
only one state. Brownness often refuses the state altogether.

My mother walked to and from high school with her
brothers and cousins. By then the girls would linger together
in a slow saunter as the boys blustered a few feet ahead. One
afternoon, at this short distance, my mother and her girl-kin
watched and screamed into the empty sky as a truck suddenly
pulled up and screeched to a halt and a group of gringo boys
leapt out with metal pipes and began beating their brothers
and cousins. *Boys like that who'd kill your brother.*

Her memory fades to black when I ask what happened next.

She chooses instead to remember what happened between the divided lines of boys and girls dancing the Stroll, how that empty space between the lines would fill with their bodies, one after the other, moving to the music, how so many of the dance moves she would show off down that line trained her to move the top of her body in one direction while the bottom half pulled in its opposite.

After Bernardo dies at the hands of Tony, Anita and Maria circle the bed for a duet. Anita may have just sung a song about the merits of "America," but now she's warning Maria about "A Boy Like That," commanding Maria to *stick to your own kind*. Maria will not be moved, insisting and insisting in her clear soprano, "I Have a Love," until Anita is moved to sink onto the bed in tortured contemplation. Through the course of their intimate duet, Anita is moved to supplant her loyalty to Bernardo with her loyalty to Maria. This move marks Anita as the only female character in the musical to prioritize her allegiance to another woman over her ties to a male romantic partner. She's moved to change her mind, to have a change of heart.

She's the only character in the musical who moves, and is moved, in this way.

Anita doesn't just move distinctly, singularly, consequentially as a dancer; she moves in these ways as a character across the musical's story. Following the duet, Anita confesses to Maria that Chino has a gun and is looking to exact revenge against Tony to honor Bernardo. Maria begs Anita to help her protect Tony. Anita agrees to deliver a message to Tony at Doc's Drugstore, the Jets' headquarters, assuring him that Maria will meet him later so that they can escape from the city together.

Alone, Anita ventures across the boundaries of turf. She's the only character in the musical who does.

Anita crosses the border into enemy territory. When she

arrives at the drugstore, the Jets verbally harass her, refusing to believe she is there to help Tony. Their animosity escalates quickly toward predatory menace until they pounce upon her and rape her. She moves beyond the boundaries that seek to enclose her and her own kind, and her body bears the physical and emotional costs often inflicted on brown women who dare to cross borders. It's not just this shared experience of violation that makes us brown girls feel for Anita, makes us feel so brown with her. It's how she moves in response to it, how she opens her mouth in the aftermath and scorches the earth.

Anita doesn't just pull the musical from song to dance, from ensemble to solo; she doesn't just move across the story; she transforms the story from comedy into tragedy. Unlike in *Romeo and Juliet*, where the star-crossed lovers meet their demise as a result of a missed message from a detained Friar, in *West Side Story*, the tragic end is summoned by the lie Anita tells in response to the violence inflicted on her. After the rape, she seethes: *I got a message for your American buddy. You tell that murderer that Maria's never going to meet him. You tell him that Chino found out about them and shot her. She's dead!* She slams the door shut as she makes her exit. She survives the violence inflicted upon her. She moves beyond our sight. She's emerged as the most powerful character in the show by delivering a curse that brings about *a plague o' both your houses.*

Anita moves across the battered gymnasium floor, across the rooftop, across the borders of crew and genre, and shows us brown girls how to make our way through the spaces we often find ourselves bound within or toward the spaces that have been denied us. She shows us how to move and move and keep on moving, how to move past the violence done to our bodies, how to get down and how to feel brown doing it. Like my mother making her way down the cleared dance floor space between her kinfolk lined up for the Stroll, showing off the moves she'd learned and the spectacular moves she'd just made up before folding herself back into the pulsing brown crowd.

Can you see her? Keep watching. Watch it with us. We'll pull back the covers. There's room enough in the bed for all of us.

Following Tony's death, Maria, in a grieving rage, grabs the gun from Chino, and wields it wildly at the Jets and Sharks who surround her, shouting, *How many bullets are left, Chino? Enough for you? And you? All of you? We all killed him; and my brother and Riff. I, too. I can kill now because I hate now.* She collapses into sobs as the police enter and attempt to retrieve Tony's dead body. Maria commands, *Don't touch him!* and silently encourages the Jets and Sharks to come together to carry Tony's body away. The two groups are at last united through shared violence and grief and incorporated into a world irrevocably shattered by the tragic aftermath of hate.

But where is Anita?

While she clearly expresses her contempt for the Jets at the end of the rape scene, Anita is not visually incorporated into the world of hate represented at the musical's end. Her absence in this final scene is in many ways no surprise, but the logical ending for a brown diva who has spent much of the musical defying the apparent limits of its narrative and choreographic boundaries. She has moved across the borderlines of turf, she has moved singularly in group dance numbers, she has moved her allegiances, so why shouldn't she move beyond the broken world staged in the closing scene?

Anita was the only Hispanic character I ever played who had a sense of dignity, who had a sense of herself, who was courageous, Moreno will recall decades later. *Anita defended herself in the ways she should have. She took care of herself.*

In the end, Anita continues to move beyond the borders of where she is supposed to be. She's not here. Not there. Perhaps she's at home. Perhaps she's singing and dancing in her bedroom. Perhaps she's elsewhere. Anita remains both of and apart from *West Side Story*, singularly plural, insisting like so many of us brown folks, on being "queer for Uncle Sam," on creating a space of belonging *and* difference. *Ni de aquí, ni de allá.* A (no) place for us.

4

Diva Comeback
Tina and the River

Back when Tina Turner was Anna Mae Bullock and attending Sumner High School in St. Louis, Missouri, she would regularly cross the Mississippi River to hear live music at nightclubs in East St. Louis, Illinois. Crossing the river meant crossing state lines and states of mind; it meant crossing toward the beginnings of her life as Tina Turner. It was at the Manhattan Club in East St. Louis where she first heard Ike Turner play with his band, Kings of Rhythm. During an intermission one night in 1957, so the story goes, Anna Mae grabbed the mic and sang B. B. King's ballad, "You Know I Love You," impressing Ike enough to eventually secure her place as a vocalist for the band. She spent the next year finishing high school and crossing the river every weekend to sing with the band at their regular gigs. By 1960, she had moved across the river to live with Ike in East St. Louis and to begin in earnest her training as a singer. That year, the band's demo of "A Fool in Love" featuring Anna Mae singing lead caught the attention of Juggy Murray, president of Sue Records, who bought the rights for the song and insisted that the band make Anna Mae its star. In response, Ike renamed Anna Mae as Tina Turner and trademarked the name, ensuring that should she ever leave him or the band, he could replace her with another Tina Turner. When Tina expressed reservations about the terms of their relationship, Ike responded by striking her in the head with a wooden shoe stretcher. She had made a crossing from which it would be nearly impossible to cross back.

The first time my father crossed the river was in the same year that Anna Mae grabbed the mic and sang the blues. It was January 1957, and he was just seven years old. He joined his mother and four of his siblings, traveling north from Mexico across the Rio Grande to settle in San Antonio, where his dad had come the year before to find work. My father grew up west of another river—the San Antonio—which he would regularly cross in 1970 as he headed east each day across town toward the army base to report for duty or dental-assistant training classes. By the time he'd crossed the Pacific and the South China Sea in 1971, the banks of the Perfume River just north of Phu Bai, Vietnam, were soaked with the blood of the many lost in the infamous Battle of Hué. His first night in Phu Bai, just 30 miles south of the DMZ, he slept through the rocket shelling and the shouting of his bunkmates hustling their asses to the nearby bunker. He never lost a minute of sleep worrying about the way things might have been. He never was the type to dwell on the losses that accompanied all the crossings he was forced to make.

Listen to the story, now, Tina instructs in the iconic spoken intro to her version of "Proud Mary." Her voice, a lure cast, breaks the stilled surface and plunges us into the deep.

The original version of "Proud Mary"—a country-rock anthem propelled by a steady percussive backbeat and twangy guitar—was written by John Fogerty and recorded by his band,

Credence Clearwater Revival, in 1968. The song was released on their album *Bayou Country* the following year and peaked at Number 2 on the *Billboard* Hot 100 chart in March. Upon receiving his military discharge notice, Fogerty was inspired to write the song about a worker who leaves a good city job for a riverboat adventure and never looks back.

> *I was still in the Army Reserve and was concerned about being sent to Vietnam. One day in the early summer of '68, I saw an oversize envelope on the steps of our apartment building. It was my honorable discharge. In the blink of an eye, I was a civilian again. I did a handstand and flipped a few times on the small lawn out front.*

The song is a declaration of escape, an epic hymn of the protagonist's journey across the water aboard the riverboat *Proud Mary*. The speaker is an itinerant laborer who's washed a lot of dishes in Tennessee and *pumped a lot of 'tane down in New Orleans* (though some quote and sing this lyric as *pumped a lot of pain*—either way, it's all labor just the same) and has left these earthbound routines behind in search of other rhythms by which to move.

Ike hated the song. But Tina heard something in it. Upon listening to the more up-tempo, Phil Spector-produced cover of the hit by the integrated R&B band The Checkmates, Ike was persuaded to record a version in 1970. Tina recalled, *We made that song our own. I loved the Credence version, but I liked ours better after we got it down, with the talking and all. I thought it was more rock 'n' roll. That was the beginning of me liking rock music.* "Proud Mary," recorded with Tina's signature prelude, became Ike and Tina Turner Revue's biggest hit, debuting on their 1970 album, *Workin' Together*, and earning them a Grammy Award for Best R&B Vocal Performance in 1972. Their concert album, *What You Hear is What You Get—Live*

AMERICAN DIVA

at Carnegie Hall, includes a twelve-and-a-half-minute-long
encore version of the song.

Listen to the story, now.

My father left a good job in the city, working as a manager
at a shoe store, when he got his draft notice and set off for
basic training in April 1969. After the drill sergeant told the
new draftees that they were all headed to infantry and sug-
gested that they could enlist for an extra year to try for a better assignment, my father signed up for medical training so
he could be stationed back home in San Antonio at Fort Sam
Houston for a spell before heading to war. He tried at first to
be an X-ray technician, and when that didn't work out he was
assigned to what the army called "casual duty," which basi-
cally meant he spent his time cleaning latrines, serving as a
night watchman, and cutting grass and raking leaves around
the grounds of the base. Just a few of the varied jobs he would
take on over the years.

In the end, my father opted for dental-assistant training
and was stationed in Petaluma, California, for a year before
getting his orders to serve in a dental detachment in Phu Bai in
March 1971, the same month Ike and Tina's version of "Proud
Mary" peaked at Number 4 on the *Billboard* Hot 100 chart.
By then, as he tells it, he'd already fallen hard for Tina after
watching her in a blur of gold fringe on *The Ed Sullivan Show*
in January 1970.

That first night in Phu Bai was, my dad recalls, *the last night
I ever slept through any kind of sound.* His ears quickly and forever
attuned to the tremors of impending arrivals—distant chop-
per blades cutting through the torpid sky, thunder's low roll,
the prickled silence just before a blast. And in the off-hours he
and his bunkmates cushioned the air around their unit with the
sounds of Jimi Hendrix, Janis Joplin, Isaac Hayes, Santana, James
Brown, Credence Clearwater Revival, and Ike and Tina Turner

Revue from albums they ordered through the post exchange. Near the banks of the Perfume River, my father learned how to listen like prey while listening to Tina sing "Proud Mary." Maybe he heard in her the sound of a fellow traveler, the sound of someone whose voice and gestures were shaped by an ear trained to sense the quality of the air just before an ambush. "Proud Mary" was a song that trained my father's ears, like Tina's, toward a fierce and practiced vigilance. A song he carried with him as he crossed the rivers and seas on his journey home.

A diva's voice possesses the power to elevate a song into a diva anthem by carrying both struggle and perseverance, both trauma and triumph within its timbre or tremolo or stretched

Tina Turner on The Ed Sullivan Show

notes or soaring range or nice-and-rough stylings. Divas sing the bloodshed and the victory. It's what Tina's voice does to "Proud Mary." Ike and Tina's five-minute-long version of "Proud Mary" traverses distances in tone, tempo, vocal stylings, and genre that the original Credence Clearwater Revival version—in its three minutes of steady-rhythmed roots rock— never did. It starts with Tina's spoken proclamation of her signature nice and rough style, a map for the route the song will follow. High-hat slaps and Ike's baritone and blues guitar float below her words. And, just as promised, Tina wades through the first verse in a soulful stroll, the Ikettes joining in to harmonize with her voice or with Ike's responses to Tina's calls when the chorus comes around. Nice and easy.

And then the blare of those Memphis soul horns. And the tumbling drums. And Tina's full-throated rasp and wail churning the surface into waked foam. And Ike's voice left behind on the shore as Tina plunges in again.

It's classic repetition with revision in the second round: Tina repeating the opening verses, only this time with the speed and force of frenetic funk, with wild abandon and complete control, with gestures of unmatched originality, of ownership. Like a diva often does when she sings a cover, Tina lays claim to it, making the song forever hers. She doesn't so much cover the song as uncover and plumb its hidden treasures. Tina's voice calling out in a low growl or spiraling shriek, calling out with clear diction on a lyric and with improvised shouts of shattered language; the Ikettes responding in propulsive harmony—*Du-Du-Du-Du-Du-Du-Du*. Nice and rough. *Tina Turner's "roughness," we discover, Francesca Royster notes, is quite labor-intensive.* Her song is soaked in sweat and river mud, undulating like a caught fish meeting air, swift and strong as the current pulled toward the sea and its great expanse.

My father returned after a year in Vietnam with his stacks

A closed loop

of LPs and a silver Sanyo reel-to-reel player he had picked up in Saigon. He spent those early days threading the machine with blank reels and recording his favorite songs from the records he'd brought back, each song a carefully laid crumb, a trail he followed to find his way back. *I was / so utterly bereft. Yet not alone— / I knew a woman's voice was saving me*, Rafael Campo recalls in his poem, "Diva." This is how I came to know my father. And Tina. How I came to know how, on most days, he could only be reached by the sound of her voice. The tape threaded from one reel to another. A closed loop.

My father came home from the war and played "Proud Mary" loud enough for the cheap drywall to shake. The horns blaring—a staff parting the waters for Tina's voice to lead the forsaken in the crossing. The horns blasting the song in half, dividing time into before and after, picking up speed until all my father could hear was the sound of never going back. All that brass unabashed in its entrance like mariachis sweeping into the rented hall of all those Mexican wedding receptions that filled our Saturday nights. Maybe that's what drew him to it, the trumpets raised, this familiar announcement of union and reunion. Or maybe all those horns, lifted and swaying together in soulful unison—nothing like the solitary bugle raised in elegy—sounded simply like survival.

Of course, it wasn't just the sounds of the horns or Tina's

voice that kept my father coming back for more, but the way
Tina moved her body through and beyond the song. That gold
fringe shuddering into sunlit waves on *The Ed Sullivan Show*
back in 1970 was, after all, what first caught his eye. For that
performance, Tina foregoes the intro and instead she and the
Ikettes dance for the first full minute of their three-and-a-
half-minute act before Tina starts singing. "Proud Mary" is
known as much for its choreography as for its rasp and blare.
Tina's performance style, her physical repertoire, is a large
part of what marks her distinctive diva persona, what makes
her so *quotable*, performance scholar Madison Moore observes,
something that she owned and which was her own fierce labor.

  To know the song is to know the moves. How did I come
to know them? It seems like I always did. As if through osmo-
sis, my father the porous border through which she passed
her nourishment onto me. The speakers trembling from the
rasp of her voice and my father safe inside the sound and me
listening from my bedroom, arms faking a freestyle with my
long braids tossed to and fro, learning how to move through
the cresting waves. Tina's choreography in "Proud Mary"
was the first diva move I ever tried to copy. I was trying to
move through the aftermath of war. The diva calls us to follow
her steps and though we can never fully achieve her greatness, we can sometimes manage to reach for our own. In those
moments, dancing alone in my room to Tina's "Proud Mary"
filling the silence between my father and me, I knew a woman's voice—and moves—were saving me.

Tina draws the nice-and-easy section of the song to a smooth
stop, the surface of the water rippling out in delicate shirrs.
Then the horns soar and the drums rumble and Tina and the
Ikettes lift their arms and spin in dervish unison. First one way
and then the other, long wisps of their wigs lifting, the hems of

their short dresses lifting, their legs as long and strong as the trunks of red maples, the banks starting to overflow from the waves made with their churning, Tina undulating in smooth shuffles across the stage and back toward the microphone. Their arms synced in rolling motions and now stretched high as they turn to profile and shatter the air with their hips rolling and now bending at the waist rolling and now diving beneath all the waves they've made rolling and now circling their arms in breaststrokes and freestyles rolling as the tempo climbs and climbs to a wild frenzy.

Royster identifies in this choreography a display of *playfully outrageous bodily knowledge*. Moore calls it *fierceness as a spastic bodily possession*. Others might see the movements of radical dissociation—a regularly practiced escape from all the forms of surveillance and violence Ike inflicted upon Tina and the others in her orbit. And I say yes. Yes, and. When Tina and the Ikettes take over all that space on the stage with their outswept arms, when they unfurl their bodies to ride every current until they have pulled us so far out, when they seem to surrender to the waves but really what they are doing is commanding them through their carefully synchronized choreography—all this abandon, all this control—when they move and move and don't stop moving in this way, what I see is not simply a form of possession, of being possessed by some higher source, but a form of taking possession. A moment—yes, fleeting, but no less real—of Tina and the Ikettes repossessing their bodies, their bonds, their artistry.

All of which is to say that what I hear and see in Tina's performances of "Proud Mary" is the process of her becoming a diva, the emergence of her *quotable* and inimitable ferocity. The labor of Tina's diva incipience inspiring so many of us to sync our own moves to hers. Perhaps that's what my father saw: a series of strokes to learn, a choreography fast-paced enough to outswim the past, to keep his head above the surface of the present while caught in the undertow of the past. I see my father and Tina doing what they had to do to survive.

In April 1972, a few months after my father's return from the war, Ike and Tina and the Ikettes performed "Proud Mary" along with a few of their other hits on *Soul Train*. On this episode, their set is broken up by an interview in which the fans pose questions to Ike and Tina. Tina smiles and fields all but one of the questions, responding with ease and the occasional glance toward Ike for reassurance, while Ike shifts solemnly beside her, exuding a sense of menacing awkwardness. A young woman named Michelle directs the first question to Tina, *Do y'all make up your own dance steps?* Tina plays demure, *Yes, between the Ikettes and myself we sort of get together and throw it together.* Her response, equivocal and dismissive, appears to downplay all the labor and creativity that she and the Ikettes poured into the making of their signature dance moves. But what I hear in it is her attempt to fashion a shield around what is rightfully hers: her body, her artistry, her connections with other women. By this time Ike had been regularly brutalizing Tina with beatings and rape and other forms of violence and terror for years. Like so many abused women, she knew to protect—to conceal by downplaying—any sign of independence or creative authority or volition or pleasure. She knew enough to appear to *sort of throw it together.* Tina had tried to kill herself by swallowing a bottle of sleeping pills back in 1968 in an effort to escape Ike's torture. Instead, she survived. She recorded and choreographed "Proud Mary."

Years later, an interviewer will engage Tina in a word association with the titles of her most famous hits. In response to "Proud Mary," Tina will say, *freedom.* Maybe that's how she saw it—how she sang it, how she danced it—for all those years. As rehearsal. As covert training drills. Maybe that's how my dad heard it. What I heard during all those years of eavesdropping on his listening was the silence and the stillness sealed inside of all that shimmy and blare.

My father came back from the war and never spoke about it. The violence was, for him, unspeakable. The only sounds of the war's lingering presence were the choked spasms of his nightly seizures. And the music he blasted from the speakers during the day. He spent much of the decade after his return threading his reel-to-reel with Stax soul and Tejano polkas and Janis Joplin's "Maybe" and Tina's "Proud Mary," turning up the volume high enough to drown out all other sounds. He was most at ease anywhere the horns blared or the cymbals crashed. At weekend weddings he taught me to spin counter-clockwise around the dance floor to Mexican polkas until the room blurred, spinning until we were each sealed so completely inside of our own centers of gravity that nothing could knock us off balance. These were our rare moments of connection. My father reaching out to me in the way that Tina had reached out to him. Through rasp and blast. Through turn and dip. Through the moves that keep you rolling down the river. Through a choreography practiced and practiced until the moves become your own.

The thing about a river is that the cliché holds. You can't step in the same river twice. Can't step out in the same place,

Father-Daughter dance

either. You can't ever really cross back to the same place you left. *For it's not the same river,* Heraclitus insists, *and he's not the same man.*

My father crossed back and took a civil-service job. After that ran its course he took a desk job working for his brother-in-law until that business went under and sometime around then or maybe sometime before—the timeline, like the riverbank, is so muddy—he scraped together enough money to buy a laundromat with two of his buddies and named it *BMW* in what seemed like a sign of immigrant aspiration but really was just an inside joke among the three of them—one Black, one Mexican, and one white guy—trying to bring in some extra cash, and through it all, long before and long after the laundromat shuttered, he moonlighted as a referee and umpire, which was in the end his favorite job, comfortable as he was on the sidelines, unafraid to make an unpopular call, thrilled by the power to call the shots, to shift an outcome, loving basketball most of all because of the ways it kept him constantly on the move, running and running, even if he was confined to the court, running alongside a team occasionally trying to run out the clock.

The night Tina left Ike for good back in Dallas in July 1976—her face swollen and cut from the heel of Ike's boot—she did not run at first. She crept. She massaged him to sleep while still dressed in a white suit splattered with her blood. *I was afraid he would hear my heart, it was beating so loud—because I knew it was time to walk.* Her head was too swollen for her wig to fit so she swathed her hair in a wrap, draped a cape over her blood-stained suit, gently covered her eyes with dark sunglasses, clasped a piece of hand luggage, tiptoed across the carpeted hotel floor, gingerly turned the knob, and eased the door shut behind her as Ike snored. She composed her body into the choreography of a casual stroll. Nice and easy. She knew she couldn't leave the way she came—through the glitteringly lit lobby—knew there was no crossing back. So, she left through a back door. It was only after she made it to the alley leading away from the Hilton, away from her contracted concert gig, away from the boot heels and the burns and the bruises and the broken bones, that she ran. *I was running by then, I was so afraid. I ran outside into an alley and threw myself in among some trash cans and just hid there for a while.* Night fell. She ran. The thirty-six cents she left with clanging in her wallet like a church bell. She moved her legs—muscled from all those spins and dips on the stage—into the stride of a sprint. She ran until the road ran out, until she reached the freeway, and then she ran across the freeway. She was nearly run over by a semi-truck, and she kept running. She ran to the Ramada Inn and held up her beaten face and asked for the manager and told him her name and promised she'd pay him back if he'd just let her stay the night. She ran toward her name. The name given to her by the man who'd rather see her dead than free. She ran into and through and over it until she made it her own. She ran and ran until she made a name for herself. *I'll just take my name*, she told the judge at the divorce proceedings when Ike refused her everything else. *That is when I realized I could use "Tina" to become a business.*

Those first months after she left, Tina hid out with friends, cleaning their houses to earn her keep. *I moved junk and stored stuff away and put out the trash and cleaned cupboards and washed dishes and scrubbed stoves—because that was the only way I could repay these people.* Months stretched to years. She kept running. Carried a .38. Cushioned the air around her with daily Buddhist chanting. Cleaned a lot of plates. Worked small-time cabaret gigs at hotels. Booked appearances on TV variety and game shows. Borrowed Bob Mackie dresses and other costumes from Ann-Margret and Cher, who helped her secure some regular gigs in Las Vegas. She took whatever job she could hustle. She worked.

Tina had met Ann-Margret back in 1970—the same year Ike

and Tina recorded "Proud Mary"—when both divas were performing in Las Vegas. After her set one night, Tina caught the end of Ann-Margret's show. In Ann-Margret's dressing room afterwards (both clad in their post-show turbans and robes), they shared their admiration for one another and became fast friends. They met again in 1974 when they co-starred in the film *Tommy*, based on the 1969 rock musical featuring the music of The Who. After the filming, Ann-Margret invited Tina—without Ike—to perform on her London-based variety show special that aired on January 23, 1975. Tina accepted the invitation. On the show, they launch their act with a short skit. They're dressed in white Victorian-style dresses, waving fans near their faces, sitting at a white table set against a white background, and surrounded by the tranquil sounds of birds chirping. They trade lines about how their fans would be surprised to see them like this—ladies of leisure who are reserved and constrained by the trappings of conventional femininity.

ANN-MARGRET: *But you and I know there's more to life than doing two shows a night, rehearsing eight hours a day, and running for planes.*

TINA [playing along]: *You are so right, and my husband Ike finally got around to seeing it that way. . . . Now I only do one show a night, I only rehearse six hours a day, and we go by train.*

[The audience laughs on cue.]

ANN-MARGRET: *Can't you just picture yourself relaxing like this from now on?*

TINA: *You mean all the time? . . . You mean no dancing?*

ANN-MARGRET: *No singing.*

TINA: *No working?*

ANN-MARGRET & TINA [leaning in toward each other, breaking character with knowing smiles, in unison]: *NO WAY!*

As the studio audience laughs, the camera cuts to the two women released from the setting of demure femininity and hard at work in their natural habitat: surrounded by stage lights, singing and dancing as they begin a free-spirited duet of Ike and Tina's hits, "Nutbush City Limits," "Honky Tonk Women," and "Proud Mary." They bond over their shared dedication to the labor, the *work*, and not the trappings of glamour, that life as a performer requires. And together they cut loose.

By the mid-1970s, diva duets—from Ethel Merman and Mary Martin in 1953 to Liza Minnelli and Pearl Bailey in 1969—had become a staple of TV variety shows. These duets delighted in bringing together divas who wouldn't otherwise share the stage, highlighting their individual distinction and shared status, and relishing the variety show's capacity for both theatrical spectacle and camera-close-up intimacy. For their duet, Tina had arrived at the taping with little more than her voice. Ann-Margret recalls, *She was having trouble with Ike, and I remember that she came there and didn't really have any of her own clothes. She is wearing my pants and a T-shirt that we found in wardrobe.* In their musical number, Tina, the long hair of her wig flowing, wears Ann-Margret's baby blue t-shirt sprinkled with white clouds, fitted blue jeans, and gray knee-high boots; Ann-Margret, her long hair loose and disheveled, wears cut-off jean shorts, a long-sleeved red t-shirt, and black knee-high boots. Their shared casual dress and easy banter conveys a sense of warmth and mutual support. Ann-Margret follows Tina's iconic choreography and, to her credit, manages to keep up, matching and fueling Tina's high-octane energy. They borrow from one another to showcase their individual prowess.

I like to imagine Tina mining Ann-Margret's wardrobe for a costume that fit. The year of the show's airing, Tina will make her first attempts to leave Ike and though she'll return to him each time, she is building up her nerve. I like to think of her inhabiting another diva's style for a moment as a way to feel closer to asserting her own. I like to think of it as a dress rehearsal for freedom.

Later that spring, Tina will perform another memorable diva duet on Cher's solo variety show, *Cher!*, for an episode that aired on April 27, 1975. It's the year before she will leave Ike once and for all and a year after Cher has split from Sonny Bono. Cher and Tina eventually became close friends, sharing their plights as divorced women who had gained fame as part of married duos and faced with enormous debts to pay from canceled joint bookings as they worked to establish themselves as solo performers. For that *Cher!* episode in April 1975, the Ike and Tina Turner Revue were the featured guests, but Ike and Tina only shared the stage once—for an opening rendition of "Nutbush City Limits," a song Tina had written. Tina performed without Ike or the Ikettes or the band in the other two acts in which she appeared, most memorably, perhaps, in her duet with Cher on Tina's cover of the Shirley & Co. song, "Shame, Shame, Shame."

The number begins with Tina dancing in long strides across the stage, showcasing her legs in a snug-fitting halter dress with floor-length fringes adorned with circular mirrored beads that capture and flash the reflected stage lights. She launches into the opening verse, her voice as nice and rough as a lioness lifting a cub in her clenched jaw. Cher enters with a shriek from stage right and joins Tina on the end of the chorus shaming the men who can't keep up with their dancing. They shuffle and strut and back-step side by side, crossing apart and coming together with hip bumps, volleying verses in their color-coordinated halter-fringed-and-mirrored dresses. They alternate between singing out to the audience and singing with playful ease directly to one another, a sense of boisterous encouragement flowing between them. Tina snarling and smiling effortlessly on every syllable; Cher audibly out of breath well before the end. But that's all right because Tina's helping her out the way a mama cat gently dangles her young from her mouth, carrying her toward the finish.

Cher and Tina affirm a sense of sisters-doing-it-for-themselves in their complementary costumes and choreography and alto registers as they come together to shame the men who can't keep up, and who can't dance, either. Their duet a glittering and raucous fuck you to Ike and Sonny. Both women working their asses off to work off the debts—material and emotional—they accrued from the trappings of marriage. What's more, the performance, marked by Tina's roar and strut, is an enunciation and confirmation of dancing as Tina's freedom language, of her creative (and therefore potentially threatening) force. She shakes her shoulders, stretches her arms wide, leans her torso back as she saunters in long zoot-suiter strides, punctuates her heel-toe shuffles with side-kicks all while she shames the man who dares to constrain her moves. Shame on the man who tries to break her into deadened stillness. *If you really think you're fast / Try to catch me if you can.* This song-and-dance a warning flare—lightning in the sky. *When she discovers her diva-incipience*, Wayne Koestenbaum writes, *she's discovering the nature of her body*. The beginning of the end for Tina and Ike. The beginning of the beginning for Tina.

I like to think of Tina pairing up with fellow divas as a way to rehearse an alternative form of coupledom from the one that shackled her to Ike. A way of imagining herself in relation to something—and someone—better. Her diva relations helping her find her way free. And Tina, in turn, offering Ann-Margret and Cher a choreography for stretching past their own capacities, past the limits of white femininity or of their own movement repertoires. Cher will later recall how she reacted when she heard Tina would appear on her show: *And then I thought, I'm gonna have to dance with Tina Turner. Do you know what that feels like? It's like dancing with a hurricane.* The waves crash. The rivers rise.

Tina worked and worked and worked on her solo career, but even as the 1980s dawned, the recording industry still saw her as the other half of a romanticized duo. Tina needed to break the chains that bound her to Ike. She never was the type to dwell on the losses that accompanied all the crossings she had made. Never lost a minute of sleep worrying about the way things might have been. But she needed to get all the way free. So, she agreed to tell her story. Pumped a lot of pain.

The December 7, 1981 issue of *People* magazine featured the interview in which Tina first made public her story of the years-long abuse, torture, and rape she suffered at Ike's hands. It wasn't the cover story. She wasn't a big star, and stories like hers were still considered best kept as open secrets. Just a small headline—among others about Candice Bergen "married at last" and cures for holiday hangovers—that read, "Tina Turner: on the prowl without Ike." The article inside the magazine introduced her as *Tina Turner: the woman who taught Mick Jagger to dance.* But for those who read on, Tina's voice and story eventually rise to the surface. She wasn't so much interested in proclaiming herself a survivor as in asserting herself as a solo act. She wanted to work.

Three years after the *People* interview, she released the album *Private Dancer,* in what many hailed as the greatest comeback of all time. Her story funneled easily into the classic diva comeback narrative: she'd endured long enough to make waves, to catch them for a stretch, to have been toppled by their force, striding back in after a lengthy spell on the shore, and, against the odds and at middle age, defiantly riding the waves again and with such impeccable form. The rasp. The hair high and spiked. The legs going all the way up to her unharnessed throat. But Tina knew there was no coming back from some things. For it's not the same river, and she's not the same woman. When asked years later about *Private Dancer*, she will say: *I don't consider it a comeback album. Tina had never arrived. It was Tina's debut.*

Tina's debut shows us how divas don't just offer lessons in the comeback but complicate the very notion of coming back. Tina's debut teaches us that sometimes there's no coming back from the long durée of violence. There's only new crossings to make. Tina's debut is Tina in full diva fruition, built in large part from the labor and discipline she rehearsed in "Proud Mary" and from the support of her diva relations. Tina shows us that it's never too late to become a diva.

She sold millions of records. Released seven successful singles from the album. Won four Grammys. Became the first female rock star to sell out stadiums across the world. Starred as Aunty Entity, the sublime Empress of a post-apocalyptic outpost in the 1985 action film *Mad Max Beyond Thunderdome*—a role created specifically for her. But in interview after interview all anybody ever wanted to talk about was Ike and the suffering she had endured at his hands. For *Private Dancer*'s closing track, Tina covers David Bowie's song "1984," her voice scratching its warning: *The times they are a-telling / And the changing isn't free.*

She wanted to get all the way free, to build a dam strong enough to stop the flow of this constant questioning. She co-wrote her autobiography *I, Tina*, with journalist Kurt Loder, in 1986, detailing her life and career with Ike. She had thought, perhaps, that getting the story out in elaborated, self-authorized detail would help her move more freely, unfettered by questions about the past. Instead, the story clung to her, a drowning body threatening to pull her under.

I'm not so thrilled about thinking about the past, and how I lived my life. It was made a story. The story was actually written so that I would no longer have to discuss the issue. I don't love that it's always talked about, you see. I made a point of just putting the news out to stop the thing so that I could go on with my life.

The thing about a story is that it's not a river, nor a boat you can hitch a ride on to flee what you're trying to leave behind. The story itself doesn't secure escape. *First you must get the story out of yourself,* the war veteran and storyteller Grey Eagle Ken Jackson would advise trauma-struck soldiers. *And then get yourself out of the story.* Hard as she worked, fast as she danced, Tina couldn't get herself out of the story. The world around her was unwilling to pass up the opportunity to dwell on a Black woman's suffering, insisting she pump a lot of pain for the benefit of our absolution or arousal. *It's like when soldiers come back from the war,* her second husband, Erwin Bach, would later reflect on how those years of interviews inflamed her post-traumatic stress.

Listen to the story, now.

In the opening credits to *Mad Max Beyond Thunderdome,* Tina sings: *You've got ten more thousand miles to go / Because you're one of the living.* Early on in the film, Tina as Aunty Entity surveys her domain: a settlement named Bartertown that generates its energy from methane produced by pig feces. *All this I built. Up to my armpits in blood and shit.* For the role, Tina donned a 120-pound chain-mail dress designed by Nancy Moriceau that was cut high up her thighs, layered with triple-tiered shoulder pads, and composed of soldered dog muzzles, butcher aprons, chicken wire, coat hangers, and other metallic detritus. Hanging from her ears were giant coiled-spring earrings that framed her head and transformed her into a silvery Afro-futurist bighorn ram-in-shining-armor. Her chain-mail clinks. Earrings sway. She locks horns and dominates her foes all across the shit-strewn, dystopic desert. Tina bore the weight of all that soldered metallic trash, made it look like couture, when really, perhaps, what she wanted was to lay it all down.

My father came back from the war and kept his story to himself. He couldn't—or wouldn't—get the story out of him-

Tina Turner as Aunty Entity

self. His silence is the current that pulled me toward writing and toward Tina. Perhaps my father heard in Tina's story a cautionary tale. Like her, he didn't much consider her fame in the 1980s a comeback because he had never stopped listening to her voice. Also, like her, he knew there was no coming back from some things. He turned up the volume on the stereo. Plugged in his headphones as he made recordings none of us could listen in on.

In his seventies, my father will lose much of his hearing. I'm not sure if this is a mercy or a curse. The story I tell is the story around his silence, which is, of course, not his story. He listened so hard for so long. As evening sets, he turns off his hearing aids. Tunes it all out. Sleeps soundly in the silence. In their final scene together Aunty Entity laughs triumphantly as she stands over Max, sparing his life. *Ain't we a pair, raggedy man?* She turns her back on him and laughs again. *Goodbye soldier*, she says, before riding off into the desert sunset. Sand clouds lift and blur the screen in the wake of her departure. She speeds away, out of the story.

5

Diva Monstrosity
Divine and Jaime

The Texas mountain laurel blossoms that perfume the air every March are beginning, like ruffled ingenues, to wither in the heat. It's late spring of 1988, and I'm a junior in high school who's managed to stay out late enough to head over to Jaime's house when the party is just getting started. Jaime is a year older and fresh-faced and preppy-pressed and gay and a freak like the rest of us. He wears blazers and belts his jeans, his thick red hair parted to the side and falling just long enough to brush his eyelashes. He is artfully composed. I can't remember if he was in the closet because when he was with us—the drama kids—he was himself.

Jaime's parents are out of town again, and he's set out the usual array of Jell-O shots and weed and wine coolers and cheap tequila. I am sober and still a virgin and sunken into the sofa as a VHS of John Waters's 1972 cult film, *Pink Flamingos*, plays on the television screen. It's the final scene: Divine sitting on the pavement eating dog shit in a trashed-up bouffant coif shaved to the earline, eyebrows arched into a sinister V.

She swallows and sneers and I feel my insides turn out. The only way I can think to describe it is to say, as we do in Chicana Spanish, *Me da asco*, which translates roughly to *It disgusts me* or *It makes me nauseous*. But *asco* is more than that—to experience *asco* is to surrender to an entanglement with the abject and the particular illuminations and transformations such an encounter provokes. I watch Divine eat the shit and I open my mouth. *What is that?* is all I can ask. Watching is all I can do, watching in the way we watch bodies pulled from mangled cars. The way, years later, I will watch as my friend Regina Jean pushes the baby out while I hold her trembling thigh, startled at how much blood and shit is involved in our acts of becoming.

I don't remember the first time I met Jaime, only who we became afterwards. I was Catholic and crooked-toothed, couldn't do splits nor contour my cheeks with blush. I moved restlessly at the edges of these confines, desperately curious to inhabit my body in pleasurable ways beyond them. Jaime moved with élan and droll irreverence, godless and godlike. Ours was an encounter marked by my curiosity and by his capacity to withstand my worship. He lived in a world of flamboyance and fisting, of casual talk about how a veined cock could make you bleed and make you come. I became alive as his witness and his pupil. As his friend.

I was a girl learning how to give and get good head. He was a boy who cruised the strip on Austin Highway. I stumbled; he strutted. Jaime was a year older than me and ages wiser. He was my diva mentor. What we shared was a desire to eat the world, to refuse its denials. We were of the generation who had been born—he in 1969 and I in 1970—into a world of promise and revolution. Jaime was born the same year that Cyclona (the drag alter-ego of queer artist Robert Legorreta) was born at Belvedere Park in East Los Angeles in the performance *Caca-Roaches Have No Friends*, written by Gronk, a fellow avant-garde Chicano artist. For the play, Cyclona wore a fur ascot, black nightgown, white face paint, bright lipstick, and simulated orgies across the stage. At the climax, generally called the "cock scene," Cylona's shirtless boyfriend appeared onstage with two eggs and a water balloon attached to his crotch. Cyclona knelt, caressed the balloon, popped it, and then smashed the eggs against the stage floor. In response, stunned and outraged audience members set the park's trash cans on fire.

Jaime and I were born into this world of raucous possibility that by the time we'd reached young adulthood we knew was not to be. By the time I saw Divine on the television set at Jaime's house in our last years of high school, we were entering the final months of Ronald Reagan's eight-year death reign. We knew the world wasn't rooting for us—the brown, the queer, the girls, the fags, the sick, the hungry. So we kept one another company, kept smoldering the erotics of our companionship and the unsentimental exchange of a deep, mutual acceptance.

Once, at another party at Jaime's house, after too many wine coolers, I stumbled my way toward an empty bedroom with my first real boyfriend, a nice-enough guy who aspired to be the next John Bonham but was really just another boy in the drumline of the marching band. In the darkened room, we kept up our stumbling toward one another. I surprised him with my sudden eagerness, pulling his dick toward my mouth for the first time, not quite sure where to put my hand and what about my other hand and how fast or how slow and how much and how to find the right rhythm and how far down my throat do I take it and how do I keep my teeth out of the way and how surprised I was at how quickly it happened—the molten jolt—so that all I could do was turn my head and throw up on the beige vacuumed carpet while still holding onto his dick with my cum-covered trembling hand. I wiped my mouth and he thanked me and we stumbled back toward the din and crush of the party.

With a friend like Jaime, a girl could talk about the gagging. About teeth and hands and cum and puke. About mechanics. About how to open the throat for movement, for new forms of expression. A diva knows how to train her throat. And those of us who worship her become who we are by opening ourselves to her full-throated expertise. At Jaime's house, I recoiled, I rejoiced, I choked, I spoke. Or, I should say, I learned to rejoice at what at first made me recoil. I learned to open my mouth to all of it—the *asco* the awe the backwash the bravado the stammering and the shrieks that startle a girl into the full range of her own voice.

During the initial run of *Pink Flamingos*, moviegoers vomited in the aisles so frequently that some theatres distributed paper sacks labelled "PINK PHLEGM-INGO BARF BAG." *You know who I am, bitch!* Divine shrieks in one scene. *I'm the filthiest person alive!* In another, she opens a gift box filled with human shit. Divine was the diva that delivered me over to my body, revealed my own sullied underside. *Divine in those days was really my Godzilla*, John Waters recalls, *a combination of Jayne Mansfield and Gorgo*. Divine was the beast who ate the beauty and then shat her out. Monstrous and abundant, her utterly, terribly human body awakening me to the miracle and filth of my very living. Awakening me as well to our shared, inevitable, and already underway decay. The shadow cast by her mythic presence was the shadow of my own mortality and of all the craven ways I wanted to live live live.

Divine was the drag alter ego of Harris Glenn Milstead, who grew up in an upper-middle-class conservative family in Baltimore. Glenn, as he preferred to be called in those days, befriended John Waters in the early 1960s, and soon they began collaborating on underground films that have since become

"I'm the filthiest person alive!"

cult classics, including *Mondo Trasho* (1969), *Multiple Maniacs* (1970), *Pink Flamingos* (1972), *Female Trouble* (1974), and *Hairspray* (1988). Beyond film, Divine performed with the avant-garde theatre troupe The Cockettes in San Francisco during the early 1970s, and by the late 1970s was a regular at Studio 54 and Andy Warhol's Factory in New York. Divine's diva persona was so outrageously and terrifyingly over-much—*a Miss Piggy for the blissfully depraved* according to *People* magazine— that he served as the inspiration for the villain, Ursula the Sea Witch, in Disney's 1989 animated movie *The Little Mermaid*. A diva for all ages. A diva for the ages.

The first time I saw Divine, *me da asco* and I felt exhilarated and I knew there was no going back. The mountain laurel blossoms succumbed to the heat. I watched Divine swallow and sneer and then gag and spit out some shit and turn back to the camera to smile widely and wink as Jaime drifted out of the living room—ever the diva-aloof host—to get high in the sun room. Jaime's diva style was nothing like Divine's. Jaime was long and lean and buttoned up; Divine was busting out of a leopard-print tube dress. But perhaps that's why Jaime was drawn to all that scatologically divine excess. Divas can turn our insides out. Divas live out loud what our true selves are like on the inside, selves we are not yet able to fully realize or that are simply too threatened by the world to live on the outside. I grew into my own style— closer to leopard print than preppy crease—in the space between Jaime and Divine. Jaime set the stage—and set out the drinks—for my diva encounters.

A few months before I saw Divine on VHS at Jaime's house, on February 16, 1988, *Hairspray*, the latest film collaboration between John Waters and Divine, had its world premiere in Baltimore, with proceeds benefitting AIDS Action Baltimore. Divine took his mother to the premiere; critics predicted that the film would launch him into the mainstream. Nineteen days later Divine died of heart failure in his hotel room the night before he was to begin shooting a guest spot on a sitcom. *Ah but you got away, didn't you, babe,* Leonard Cohen sings of Janis Joplin, *I remember you well in the Chelsea Hotel.*

Some weekends when he was flush with cash, Jaime would rent out a room or two at the Dunes Motel for one of his parties, and we would drift in and out under a star-pocked sky, the gravel of the unpaved drive catching in our tires as we pulled away. High school was nearing its end and we were beginning to feel and to fear the possible—the precarious—destinations of our bodies' desires. We were beginning to learn about transmission, about how certain things couldn't be passed on from mosquitos or kissing or casual touch. Actual bodily fluids were involved. Blood and shit and cum.

The thing about Texas mountain laurels is that they thrive in rocky soil and often endure long spells of drought, briefly flaunting their showy blossoms with a scent so strong, so sickly, so rottingly sweet, it's as if you've entered the mouth of a chola with perfectly contoured red lips smacking and blowing on her giant wad of grape bubble gum. Their cascades of purpled clusters are a big fuck you to their inhospitable conditions.

In the years after the infamous Belvedere Park performance, Gronk joined together with three other LA-based Chicanx artists—Patssi Valdez, Harry Gamboa Jr., and Willie F. Herrón III—to form the experimental, guerilla-style arts collective *Asco.* In my favorite work, captured in a photograph taken by Gamboa, they each stand—impeccably dressed in high Chicanx slicked-back style—around the gaping hole of a storm drain. The cement wall around the darkened drain is stained brown from the accumulation of filth. Patssi's lipstick is bold and unmarred. They called this piece "Asshole Mural." I could stare into it all day.

One night sometime in the year after I graduated from high school, I joined Jaime at our friend Jenny's apartment, where we spent the evening dressed up in vintage clothes with no place in particular to go. We drank cheap wine and shared a pack of Dunhills that Jenny had splurged on or maybe swiped from the corner store. We posed in what we thought were artful ways for the camera until our eyes blinked against the red splotches left from the flash's afterimage. A VHS of Nicolas Cage and Cher falling in love in *Moonstruck* played on the television. *You can't see what you are. And I see everything. You're a wolf,* Cher proclaims before Cage knocks the kitchen table over and they embrace. We hit rewind.

Our favorite scene was when they go to the opera to see *La Bohème* and Cher cries as Cage reaches out to touch her at the climax of Mimi's aria. *I mean she was coughing her brains out. And still she had to keep singing,* Cher tearfully admires the diva as she and Cage descend the carpeted staircase at the Met. The opera diva, Wayne Koestenbaum reminds us, is often associated with disease: *The diva's voice may come shadowed in sickness, but I learn from it to revere my own derangement.* Near the end of the movie, Cage proclaims to Cher: *I'm a wolf? You run to the wolf in me—that don't make you no lamb! . . . We are here to ruin ourselves. And—and to break our hearts. And love the wrong people. And—and—die!*

Jaime was a wolf in preppy clothing. The she-wolf who raised me to ruin myself. The only photo I have of him is from that night we watched Cher cry as Mimi coughed and sang. He's wearing a white button-down oxford shirt and a tweed blazer and is standing behind the beaded curtain dividing the bedroom from the rest of the studio, his hand reaching through the veil holding a plastic cup like a chalice.

Jaime moved beyond the curtain and Divine ate the dog shit and Cher lay down with the wolf and I was never the same. The autumn came and the mountain laurel blossoms turned to darkened felt pods filled with poisonous beans the color of blood that few potential predators will touch. Divas touch the

Jaime behind the curtain

most sullied place in us, invite us to touch it ourselves, to touch
it in one another, to touch the Other. Divas say, *Live in your
sickness. Live in your wounds. Live in your most base desires even if
it might kill you. Live.*

   I don't know what happened on the other nights Jaime visited the Dunes Motel without the party's entourage. I don't
know who he told. He never told me. I don't know who he
worshipped or whose worship he sought on those nights. I just
know that Mimi's aria filled the room and I never saw him
again. None of us who were his girlfriends did. I don't know
who wiped his blood and shit at the end. I don't know the details
of those last days. Was he alone? He was too young to have had
a longtime lover. Who was there to worship him? I had never
met his parents. Was it their choice not to let us know? Was
it his? Maybe he knew that I hadn't earned the right to that
kind of access, that I had never truly known him what with all

my worship and fear and hunger getting in the way. Maybe he wanted to remain fresh-faced and preppy-pressed and artfully composed in my memory of him in one final diva act. All I know is that the names of the motels along the strip on Austin Highway—The Dunes, The Sun, The Sands—summon the landscape of the shore and that the waves come hard and fast, cresting and crashing with unrelenting force.

Oh, Jaime, I don't mean to suggest that I loved you the best. I remember you well in the Dunes Motel.

The 1980s ended. I left for college. I fucked the wrong people. Got only marginally better at blowjobs without Jaime there to guide me. I tried on occasion to ruin myself but mostly ended up ruining my night or my dress. Danced on Saturday nights with my new gay boyfriends at the Bonham Exchange Disco and spent hungover mornings reading their issues of Tom of Finland's *Kake* Comics. Crossed my fingers each month for my period to come. Took pregnancy tests and

Live in your wounds

AIDS tests and cried in bathroom stalls and threw up into friends' toilets after too much cheap tequila while my girlfriends held back my hair. I lived each day as my diva-wolf-mothers had taught me. I lived in the blood and barf and shit and cum. I lived.

6

Diva Feminism

Aretha and the Rest

It's January 19, 1993, the eve of President Bill Clinton's first inauguration, and Aretha Franklin ascends the steps to the stage of the Inaugural Gala at the Capital Centre in Landover, Maryland. This isn't her first inauguration. Nor will it be her last. She is wearing a voluminous, chocolate brown, floor-length cape bordered with a wide row of caramel-colored fur over a bright yellow ballgown—a queen bee dripping with so much nectar.

Tickets to the gala are by invitation only, but fortunately, for the rest of us, CBS is televising the event. Still, I fail to tune in. It's the first day of classes in my final semester of college, and, anyway, I've mostly forsaken TV, storing the twelve-inch black-and-white my grandmother had given me at the bottom of my closet after watching the Los Angeles police beat Rodney King in 1991 and tuning in to the press conference announcing the acquittal of the officers on the news the following spring. I had voted for Clinton—my first presidential election, having been just shy of eighteen when Bush was elected my senior year in high school. I'm young enough to believe that change might come after spending my adolescence in the death grip of the Reagan era. I'm spending my nights trying to cast *for colored girls* at my mostly white liberal arts college and wearing my grandmother's chocolate-brown rabbit fur coat even though it hasn't dipped below 40 degrees all winter. I can't yet decipher the neoliberal writing on the wall.

Of course, had I tuned in to Aretha's performance, I might have learned something about how to assess and respond to the moment we were living through, the losses we were headed toward. About how to revise the script for the role you're called to inhabit. About the persistent sounds of Black freedom dreams, lest we be fooled by the false promises of a president who would go on to gut immigrant rights and welfare and other social services after playing the saxophone on late-night TV and shaking hands in Harlem.

Aretha crosses the stage to settle herself on a stool, and the television camera cuts to a still image of her in her golden ballgown along with the title of the song she will sing: "I Dreamed a Dream." It's a song sung by the anguished and abject young female character, Fantine, from the musical *Les Misérables*, which is in the sixth year of its eventual sixteen-year original Broadway run. It's a song of despair and longing for happier days. A song of sexual and financial ruin. Of aftermath.

Or at least it was.

Franklin begins: *I had a dream.* Like an expert seamstress, she alters the original until it takes on a different shape. She's cut the first stanza. She's starting in the middle of the song. Sort of. Her slight alteration of the opening lyrics lets out the fabric of the song to make room for another story.

I had a dream, she sings. Her alterations evoke Martin Luther King Jr.'s speech at the March on Washington thirty years before, so that when she sings the original lyrics that follow about the threats of tigers and thunder and other forces that *turn your dreams to shame*, she is delivering a lament for King's unfulfilled dreams. She sings the word *shame* five times, each time stretching that long *a* to its outer limits. Each time transforming the word from a description into an indictment.

The Inaugural Gala occurs on the day after the MLK Holiday—only the eighth year of its official commemoration. Aretha's honoring the fallen leader as an instruction, as a command to the future one. Franklin launches into the fourth verse, and an all-Black gospel choir marches in to surround the elevated stage. She sings of loss, freeing one arm from her fur as she sings and lifting the back of her freed palm dramatically to her forehead, then letting the cape drop from her other arm. She turns upstage to drape the cape over the stool and returns downstage as she repeats the final phrase of the verse. Her charged movements and repeated lyrics evoking the sights and sounds of grief's longue durée.

She's downstage center now, towering over the choir, repeating and revising Fantine's lovelorn cries of abandonment into an anthem of the Black freedom struggle. Into an elegy for one of its leaders. Into an assertion of enduring presence and demands. When she sings the original lyrics about her enduring capacity to continue dreaming, she is insisting that King's dream lives on. And then, inevitably, as her singing often does, the conjuring happens. She summons the dead, her "I" capacious enough to hold all the living who are dreaming the dreams of the dead. She's standing firm, stretching out her right arm, pointing her index finger toward the audience, growling out, blasting open a portal with her dream song.

By now the choir voices are risen along with the dead. So many voices.

In the original, Fantine relinquishes herself to isolation and defeat in the closing lyrics. But Franklin keeps ripping the seams open. In the final line, Aretha shifts—like a tectonic plate causing the ground beneath us to rumble—from

Aretha Franklin, inaugurating force

first-person singular past tense to first-person plural present tense. She alters the song to insist on the perseverance of *the dreams that we dreeaamm*. The choir voices rise to meet hers. All the voices climbing higher and higher. She moves in and toward a mode of collective perseverance. The diva as a singular plurality. As an inaugurating force.

By the 1990s, Aretha Franklin was long reigning as the Queen of Soul. A national treasure. Or, as Billy Preston, her longtime piano man, would say to her biographer, David Ritz: *the best fuckin' singer this fucked-up country has ever produced*. The superlatives to describe her talent are endless and every bit earned. Her powerful and capacious voice carries the moan and the murmur, the declaration and the lingering questions, the toiled soil and the underground, the captive and the free, the blues and the church, body and soul, funk and rock-and-roll.

Born in Memphis and raised in Detroit, Aretha was both influenced by and took a large part in shaping the rich musical traditions of American music that originated and blossomed in these cities. She was the daughter of the renowned preacher Reverend C. L. Franklin, and began singing gospel music in his church as a child. By her early teens, regarded by those around her as a child prodigy, she had quit school to sing with her father's traveling gospel revival, seeking out diva education and mentorship from acclaimed singers like Dinah Washington and Clara Ward. She is perhaps best known for her enduring 1967 hits, "R-E-S-P-E-C-T," "(You Make Me Feel Like) A Natural Woman," "Chain of Fools," "Do Right Woman, Do Right Man," "I Never Loved a Man (The Way I Love You)," and for her decades-long span—more than 33 years—of charted hits. She offered to post bail for Angela Davis in 1970, proclaiming, *Black people will be free. I've been locked up (for disturbing the peace in Detroit) and I know you got to disturb the peace when you can't get no peace.*

By the time of her death in 2018, Aretha had sung at the

funerals of Mahalia Jackson and Martin Luther King Jr. and at the presidential inaugurations for Jimmy Carter, Bill Clinton, and Barack Obama (and famously declined the invitation to sing at the inauguration of Donald Trump). She was the first woman inducted into the Rock & Roll Hall of Fame, the youngest person to receive a Kennedy Center Honor, the recipient of the National Medal of Arts and the Presidential Medal of Freedom. Aretha, as Angela Davis once said of her version of "My Country 'Tis of the Thee," *is not necessarily saying that this is the land of liberty but rather that we should be inhabiting a land of liberty.* For Davis, *Aretha brought a feminist dimension, before the emergence of black feminism, to our consciousness with R-E-S-P-E-C-T.* In Aretha's voice, we can hear, as Davis insists, *a yearning for freedom.*

Two months after Aretha's 1993 Inaugural Gala performance, Karen Heller, a regular columnist for the *Philadelphia Inquirer*, launches her article, "Divas: Loud, Proud, and Fashionable," by adapting James Agee's well-known phrase: *Let us now praise famous women. . . . For now is the era of the diva.* Heller delights in what she sees as a new political era inaugurated by the public celebration of divas that, as she notes, was ushered in by dazzling appearances by Barbra Streisand, Diana Ross, and Aretha Franklin at Clinton's inaugural festivities: *the inaugural was simply one of the grandest, most bountiful displays of divahood in this nation's proud history.*

This grand display of divas and their accoutrements of excessive femininity (ball gowns and painted nails and voluminous furs) signaled for Heller the triumph of a certain kind of female power that until then had been punished or pathologized. *Divas are the overhead smash to the backlash*, she asserts. Her reference to backlash is an unmistakable nod toward Susan Faludi's 1991 book, *Backlash: The Undeclared War against American Women.* As the overhead smash to this backlash against feminism, divas have apparently ascended as the new symbols

of female and, more specifically, feminine empowerment. To
celebrate divas, Heller insists, is to mark the end of the backlash era, to hail the assertion of a markedly feminine display of
female power, to talk about feminism without actually speaking its name. Which is to say that divas emerge in this moment
as paragons of a postfeminist sensibility, of a simultaneous
embrace and repudiation of feminist ideals.

Diva, it seemed, was now the word to use when you wanted
to avoid but still flirt with the f-word. Don't worry, Heller
assures us, even as a diva is a virtuosic performer, she is as well
an attainable role. Heller even offers a few "How-To" tips for
our own diva makeovers through acts of excessive accessorizing like wearing big coats and buying fancy jewelry rather than
studying music or running for office or raising our voices in a
chorus with other divas. No longer a label for the select, unat-
tainable, virtuosic, larger-than-life performer or public figure,
diva was now a role to access and accessorize your individual, consumerist, feminine (feminist?) power. A new era was
dawning in which diva emerged as the consummate mode of
gendered self-disciplining in the name of self-empowerment.
Aspiring to diva status or diva style was fast becoming a prev-
alent way women were enticed into postfeminist practices of
self-surveillance and self-improvement in the guise of female
power. Let us now praise and mourn the diva as a stand-in for
feminism, as a way to simultaneously perform its role onstage
and cast it into shadow in the wings.

What was a college girl to do?

At the end of that inaugural diva spring, my grandmother
threw me a college graduation party in her cleared-out car-
port and my Aunt Julie spent the better part of the evening
flirting with my boyfriend. Julie was not yet 35 and though she
was already a stay-at-home mother picking out custom drap-

ery for her suburban home, the trappings of that life had not succeeded in taming her wild and extravagant ways. She was the heir apparent to Tía Lucia's diva indulgences and improprieties. They wore sequins in the daytime. As for me, I was just a diva-in-waiting, a witness and a willing apprentice to their whims and their waywardness.

Which is to say I was learning how to be a feminist in the early 1990s. I watched and believed every word of Anita Hill's testimony. I crossed this bridge called my back. I rolled down the windows and sang along to the blasted volume of Indigo Girls' songs. I recited poems by Lucille Clifton and Sharon Olds like scripture. I read Susan Faludi's book. I learned that my generation was apparently part of what Rebecca Walker called the *third wave*. I became intimately familiar with the aspirations and limitations of my own body in my efforts to learn Janet Jackson's "Rhythm Nation" choreography. I explored my clitoris. I finally managed to cast and stage the production of *for colored girls* for my senior theatre project. I wept in the library the first time I read Audre Lorde transform her experience of rubbing the topaz pellet sealed inside a block of government margarine into groundbreaking feminist theory in "Uses of the Erotic: The Erotic as Power."

The erotic is a measure between the beginnings of our sense of self and the chaos of our strongest feelings. It is an internal sense of satisfaction to which, once we have experienced it, we know we can aspire. For having experienced the fullness of this depth of feeling and recognizing its power, in honor and self-respect we can require no less of ourselves.

Thick dusk dissolved into dance-glistening night as Aunt Julie reached her arm around my boyfriend's waist, slipping her hand into the back pocket of his jeans, lingering for a long moment, pressing her hand against his firm ass and laughing louder than the music. And I loved her for it. *For the erotic is not a question only of what we do; it is a question of how acutely and fully we can feel in the doing.*

Within a year, I had left the boyfriend behind to start graduate school in Chicago. Not long after I arrived, Aunt Julie sent me a care package filled with flannel sheets and sexy underwear and a message written in her elegant, looping cursive: *To help you stay warm in the winter.* By the following spring, I had broken it all in, along with my dancing shoes at clubs like the Hot House and Nacional 27 and house parties where we scuffed up the hardwood floors to the sounds of Selena, La India, and Celia Cruz.

Selena Quintanilla Perez, known simply as Selena, was at the height of her career that year I *Bidi Bidi Bom Bom*-ed my way across the dance floor with my newfound girlfriends. She had established herself as the Queen of Tejano Music, known for mixing Janet Jackson–inspired moves with the tear-in-her-voice stylings of classic Mexican ranchera singers. Like me, she was a Generation X (Mex!) Mexican-American from Texas, shared a fondness for red lipstick and a danceable beat, and spoke shaky Spanish, fluent instead in Spanglish (that frequently derided borderlands language). Unlike many Tejanes like us—neither Mexican enough for the Mexicans nor American enough for the Americans—she was beloved across geographical, linguistic, musical, and generational borders. By the end of 1994, she had released four Spanish-language albums, winning a 1994 "Best Mexican-American Album" Grammy for *Selena Live!* and was nominated for a 1995 "Best Mexican American Album" Grammy for her hit-filled album, *Amor Prohibido*, that showcased her skills across musical genres from cumbias to new wave. She was selling out concerts in the United States and Mexico while wearing the sparkling costumes she designed. As the spring of 1995 neared, she was in the process of recording her first English-language album, titled *Dreaming of You.* She was our (Mexican-)American Dream.

On the afternoon of March 31, 1995, the Chicago winter was beginning its slow thaw, the weather warm enough for me to open the windows, to let it all in, so the news came fast. Selena's been shot. The Queen of Tejano Music is dead. Just two weeks shy of her twenty-fourth birthday. I was alone in my room—the flannel sheets Aunt Julie had sent me unmade on my bed—and I fell to my knees. Selena hadn't yet finished *Dreaming of You*. At her funeral on April 3rd, thousands of mourners placed white roses—her signature flower—on top of her coffin. That July, *Dreaming of You* was released and included the English-language tracks she had completed along with several of her Spanish-language hits. It becomes, and will remain for decades, the best-selling Latin album of all time. Selena: Spanglish until the end.

The next month, I found Lisa Jones's *Bulletproof Diva* on display at the Barnes and Noble Bookstore not far from campus. The book was a compilation of essays on Black style that Jones had been writing for her *Village Voice* column, "Skin Trade." *Consider this a narrative in which we invent our own heroine: the Bulletproof Diva. A woman whose sense of dignity and self cannot be denied: who, though she may live in a war zone like Brownsville, goes out every day greased, pressed, and dressed.* Jones's diva origin story: Black feminine style as the armor she fashions in the war zone in which she lives. So, even as the diva was ascending as an exemplar of postfeminist consumer power in the mid-'90s, the diva persisted—at least for one Black feminist—as a defiant role, as a regular practice of adornment and behavior that gets a girl through the day. *A Bulletproof Diva is not, I repeat, that tired stereotype, the emasculating black bitch too hard for love or piety. . . . Bulletproof Diva is whoever you make her . . . as long as she has the lip and nerve, and as long as she uses that lip and nerve to raise up herself and the world.* Even in the moment when her name was used and abused and her power diluted and dera-cialized, the bulletproof diva was managing to elude complete consumption and endure as a self-defined role—*whoever you make her*—crafted in opposition to tired stereotypes. A Black heroine in relation to other Black heroines whose style and lip and nerve were the diva superpowers that enabled her to lift as she climbed.

What was an emerging brown feminist graduate student to do? Selena was dead, and I was in need of a diva who was bulletproof. A diva who had perfected the art of giving lip and contouring it, too. I bought the book.

A diva needs to hold on to Aretha, Elizabeth Alexander writes in her verse play, *Diva Studies*, that premiered in May 1996 at the Yale School of Drama's University Theatre. It was the same spring that Warner Brothers announced an open audition casting call for their much-anticipated biopic, *Selena*, and 24,000 young Latinas showed up in glittering Selena-inspired outfits. It was a few months after Aretha had attended a performance of *Sunset Boulevard* at the Ford Centre for the Performing Arts in Toronto where her friend, the acclaimed actress Diahann Carroll, was starring as Norma Desmond. Aretha bought two tickets in the front row: one for herself and one for her mink coat. A diva does not need to hold onto her coat.

Alexander's *Diva Studies* features five divas: a diva in distress ("Diva 2") who is comforted by four others (Divas 1, 3, 4, 5). They are surrounded by a backup "Chorus." The divas are mythic and everyday: they speak of Eartha Kitt and simmered collards. They sing, they shimmy, they shimmer like celestial bodies or oil-dressed greens in the pot. About her diva study, Alexander says, *The diva certainly is and looks fabulous, but it's not only a presentational fabulousness. It's survival. Fortitude is the word I keep coming back to.* She's quoted in Alvin Klein's *New York Times* article, "Divas in Metaphor, Divas in Crisis, Divas in Life," that appeared a few days before opening night. He liked the play but doesn't lead with a reference to the playwright or details about the production. Instead, he despairs over what he sees as the current diva devaluation pervading the culture at large. *If ever a word signifying distinctiveness has been worked to death, the word is diva.* He decries the ways the term *has deteriorated to a label of convenience, gluing itself onto the plain actress in a showy role, the would-be chanteuse on the cabaret circuit and the everyday drag queen crossing the street.*

It wasn't so much that divas were in crisis (in both the play and the world), but, as the title of his review suggests, it was that the overuse of "diva" as a metaphor was causing a crisis—at least for Klein. "Diva" no longer referred exclusively to the thing itself but had become a thing that stood in for another thing, the vehicle in the metaphor rather than the tenor (or soprano in divaspeak). Diva was now a way of talking indirectly, as figurative speech does, about other things rather than standing alone in the spotlight referring to one thing and one thing only.

But what of it? Unlike Karen Heller, for whom the diva's recent expansiveness encourages assertions of feminine fabulousness for aspiring women, Klein sees an evacuation of meaning, a dissolution and not a democratization of rarefied power, in the over- or misapplication of the diva label. All of which leads Klein to a state of crisis, or at least leads him to claim that a crisis is at hand: the borders between the virtuosic anointed few and the masses of aspiring girls, would-be chanteuses, and everyday drag queens have been breached. Klein wrings and wrings his hands. It's a moment when exalting or excoriating divas was a way, and often *the* way, of making claims about women in public. Heller praises the expanding boundaries of "diva" to proclaim a (post)feminist era; Klein polices those boundaries to express alarm over the increased visibility of aspiring female and feminine figures on the stage and the street.

As for Alexander, she's not invested in nostalgic (white) ideas of diva glamour nor in diva power as feminine (consumerist)

aspiration. What interests her is diva studies rooted in a famil-
ial and larger cultural history, a Black feminist history, specifically a Black feminist history of her grandmother, Wenonah
Bond Logan. *Why was my grandmother, a social worker in New
York City, who retired in the 70's, so extraordinary and fabulous?
She knew how to read the world around her, how to navigate narrow
straits—and come up with a withering remark at any given moment.
She was competent and glamorous in a world that said black women
are not supposed to be.* Within this context, asserting a claim
to divas means accounting for the creative practices—*reading*
and *navigating* and speaking out *with a withering remark*—that
Black women like Grandmother Logan perfected into virtuosic and audacious acts of survival with style.

Alexander's lyrical dialogue captures the bold assertions of
self-definition and communal care among Black women who
understand their acts of resilience as the very source of diva
knowledge that must be proclaimed and, above all, passed on.
In this world, divaness is relational. Alexander's divas share
recipes and remedies, they hold each other close and hold
each other accountable, they gently upbraid their fellow divas'
shortcomings and braid the ailing diva's hair. Black feminine
style is the diva's power source, the weapon she uses to inhabit
fortitude with flair. Diva as Black female joyous defiance.

Diva studies, then, is the interpretive lens through which
we can see more clearly the full contours of Black women's
lives. Diva studies is a resistant and radiant conduct of Black
women's life as well as the method of recovering and making
meaning from everyday Black female acts of resiliency. Diva
studies is the set of historical practices, the recipes, handed
down, that we can only hope to follow.

The year after the premiere of Elizabeth Alexander's *Diva
Studies*, Aretha recorded her song "A Rose Is Still a Rose" at
Vanguard Recording Studios not far from her Detroit man-
sion. It's the title track from her thirty-fourth studio album

that will be released by Arista Records the following February and will earn her Grammy nominations for "Best Female R&B Vocal Performance" and "Best R&B Song." Clive Davis, head of Arista and longtime producer and supporter of Aretha, had encouraged her to collaborate with contemporary R&B and hip hop artists like Lauryn Hill and Sean "Puffy" Combs and others who would ultimately contribute to the album, which would become Aretha's biggest commercial success during the 1990s.

In 1997, Lauryn Hill had just left the Fugees and was beginning to record what would become her iconic solo album, *The Miseducation of Lauryn Hill*, that will be released the following summer and will play nonstop in my Chicago apartment for years after that. During her year of transition, Hill wrote and produced "A Rose Is Still a Rose," wisely casting Aretha as the diva mentor who counsels and consoles a heartbroken young acolyte while Hill, in her signature sampling brilliance, sings backup, repeating and revising the lyric, "What I am is what I am," from Edie Brickell & New Bohemians' 1986 hit single, "What I Am."

On the track, Aretha speaks the song's intro, offering words of comfort to a young heartbroken girl before Hill's voice and the bass line come pumping in. The song shifts and shifts its address: Aretha recounts for us the story of the girl done wrong—*She never knew what hit her, ooohh*; Aretha chastises the one who did the girl wrong; Aretha speaks directly to the girl. She has something to say to everyone. The result is a catchy anthem of resilience propelled by a shuffling beat, Aretha's elongated vowels, and Hill's steadfast supporting vocals. Hill understands that a heartbroken girl needs to hold on to Aretha's words.

On the afternoon of October 4, 1997, the leaves were turning though the weather in the Detroit area was unseasonably warm. I was on an Amtrak train near Jackson, Michigan, about an hour west of the Vanguard Recording Studios where Aretha was singing *She never knew what hit her* when it happened. At first the lurch. Strong enough to loosen the pen from my grip. The spiral notebook splayed on my lap suddenly flung against the back of the seat in front of me. Out the window a storm of corn husk—stalk and silk and ear and—I hear the braking— the breaking.

A train wreck. (AP news wire: *A pickup truck whose driver apparently didn't see an Amtrak passenger train coming was hit and pushed a mile along the tracks in Grass Lake Township, Mich., before the train came to a stop*). The screech and stall. *A firm terrible*, Gertrude Stein once wrote, *a firm terrible hindering*. Train wheels sparking against the tracks. The truck's cab split by the impact from the trailer spewing its haul of corn across the prairie.

After the lurch and the lash, the sprint. Run-stumbling along the tracks with others away from the wreckage, dragging my suitcases—*a firm terrible hindering*—dragged down by the weight. We wait in the field until we're taken to another holding station. We wait for the crash to clear. We wait for the next train. My journal entry scribbled frantically in the waiting: *My body aches from carrying all this baggage. When will I learn my lesson? When will I learn what to hold onto and what to let go of?*

It's in the time before anyone I know has a cell phone so I can't reach my mother until late that night once I'm finally back in Chicago.

There's been an accident.
She is telling me.
Yes, I know, I say. *But I am OK.*
There's been an accident.
She is repeating herself.

Yes. But I'm—
There's been an accident. Julie is dead.

I max out the meager limit I have left on my credit card and board a plane. I return to Texas for the services and agree to take on the task of cleaning out Julie's closet and dresser drawers. This is how I end up entering the inner sanctum of a diva's boudoir. The walk-in closet was built for two, but Julie had taken over all of it. The racks thick with *orange butterflies & aqua sequins*, as Shange writes in *for colored girls*. I bury my face in it—the cashmere and polyester, the denim and lamé—for what seems like entire afternoons. It brings me to my knees. On the closet floor around me, bags and bags of clothes in all sizes with the tags still on. Julie always fluttered, moving too fast to be bothered with dressing rooms at the stores she frequented, so she often bought multiple sizes to try on back at home. Sometimes she'd remember to return the ones that didn't fit. Sometimes she'd keep the smaller sizes if she was in an aspirational mood. Sometimes they all just stayed in the bag. Inevitably, the bags would pile up, credit limits be damned. What can I say? Sometimes, divas die owing. I wonder if Aretha ever paid back those unpaid taxes or overdue bills to Saks Fifth Avenue for all the pumps and furs that lined her closets.

The drawers are filled with sealed packets of unopened stockings. Oh, Julie, I weep, how did your pantyhose outlast you? I empty it all out. The drawers and the hangers and the laundry baskets and the shoeboxes and the shopping bags. I throw heaps into plastic garbage bags and pile them in the car for Goodwill. I drive and drive and drive the loaded car along miles of highway. Weeks pass. I donate the bags eventually but I can't remember when or where. All I recall are the long stretches of road ahead of me.

I wander the nearby mall. I'm nearing thirty and have only ever properly learned the broad and garish strokes of stage makeup. So, I let the cosmetic attendants at the Chanel counter show me how to contour my lips. I spend a sizable portion of my monthly student stipend check on Vamp lipstick. I wear it every day. Tell myself that I, too, can be bulletproof. *Tossin' and flossin', tryin' to fill the void heartbreak brings*, Aretha sings about the distraught girl. I apply the lipstick. I look good. I'm a diva. I bounce checks on more makeup. I hate myself. I smile at my made-over reflection. I am so desperately sad. I wear the lipstick. *Melancholy do lip sing*, Gertrude Stein writes in her poem "Sacred Emily," observing the everyday actions of a solitary woman.

Aretha released "A Rose Is Still a Rose" in February 1998 while I was still in Texas feeling depressed and avoiding my dissertation. It was a big month for her. At the Grammys on February 25th, she performed "R-E-S-P-E-C-T" at the awards ceremony and returned to her dressing room to find one of the show's producers waiting for her with news that Luciano Pavarotti had to cancel and could she replace him in twenty minutes? She said yes. The arrangement wasn't even in her key. She returned to the stage in her red brocade dress trimmed by a mink collar and cuffs and caressed every last word of Puccini's aria, "Nessun dorma," with her remarkable voice: *Vincerò! Vincerò! Vincerò!* She was just shy of 56 years old and her voice endured—embattled, perhaps—in the sound of the future: suffused with our deepest wishes for what's on the horizon, snuffing out any doubts of endurance. *Rose is a rose is a rose is a rose*, Stein writes. Or as Aretha assures us, "A Rose Is Still a Rose."

The month after Aretha's legendary Grammy performance, a sold-out crowd gathered at the Beacon Theatre in New York City on April 14, 1998 for VH1 Divas Live. The much-anticipated event was the first in what would become a series of annual pop-diva-studded concerts that benefit "Save the Music," a nonprofit foundation launched by VH1 to help restore music education programs in public schools. The concert was being filmed live for VH1 and would become the highest rated program in the network's 13-year history, with an estimated 20 million viewers. This inaugural concert featured performances by Mariah Carey, Gloria Estefan, Shania Twain, Celine Dion, and Aretha Franklin. They were joined by singer-songwriter Carole King. Each diva was introduced by a white actress: Jennifer Aniston, Teri Hatcher, Sarah Jessica Parker, Susan Sarandon.

But before the divas sing, there are announcements and demonstrations of the event's premise and purpose: divas are swooping in to save the school music programs slashed by the state. It's a bird! It's a plane! No, it's a diva—whose singularity is her superpower and who's sponsored by the private sector— here to save the day or at least the music from neoliberal policies that are emptying resources from public schools.

Cut to a video showing scientific research about the value of music education. Cut to a video of interviews with unnamed Black children in a music room talking about how music helps them learn math. Cut to a video of Michael Walker, a Black music instructor, expressing his gratitude: *We could not have accomplished this if it wasn't for "Save the Music" in our schools which donated this [turns briefly to run his fingers along the keys] fabulous piano for us.* Watch the mostly white audience clap.

Cut to a video of President Bill Clinton, First Lady Hillary Rodham Clinton, and John Sykes, president of VH1, seated together, Hillary speaking: *I'm honored to join the President, John Sykes, tonight's performers, and all of you to "Save the Music" in our nation's schools. While most of us will never sing like Aretha Franklin or Celine Dion, an education in the arts can help all of us reach our individual dreams. . . .* Oh, the phrases and grammar of neoliberal obfuscation. The very culprits of cutbacks to

public services smile on the screen attempting to deflect attention away from the government's role in cutting these very
programs by praising the private sector and the special indi-
viduals—divas and donors like us—for taking on the responsi-
bilities abandoned by the state.

John Sykes speaks next, explaining how President Clinton has
generously offered to donate his spare saxophone to the cause.
Enter Gregory Thompson, a Black teenaged musician. The
president stands and magnanimously presents the saxophone
to Gregory, who thanks the president for the gift. Giveth the
saxophone with one hand and taketh the programs in which to
learn how to play it with the other. It's a bird! It's a plane! It's the
receding hairline of the diminished public sphere in the guise of
the exalted white savior accompanied, as always, by the grateful
Black child and by a lineup of divas—as late twentieth-century
icons of neolibualist individualist ideals—waiting in the wings.

Cut to the audience applauding and awaiting the return of
the divas. Alexander: *And so the divas scramble.*

POETIC INTERLUDE
*Composed entirely of headlines and pronouncements from
popular news articles that appeared between January 1998
and December 1999*

You've Come a Long Way, Diva.
Are we in the midst of a diva devaluation? You have to
Be able to back up being a diva with some history.
Classic divas were powerful women who didn't need
    business suits. Alas,
Diva takes a dive. Diva lingo: Destination Diva, Discount
    Diva, Dishy Diva, Diva'd to Death.
Everywhere you turn, there's another new diva on the
    scene. Even some
Feminists have gotten in the act. Now that diva has

Gone mainstream, why not have fun with the concept?
How do you know who's really a diva and who's not?
Is everyone a diva in disguise? You don't have to be a
     superstar to be a diva—you
Just have to think you are one. You just
Know. You can't leave the house just
Looking like everybody else. God forbid. You
Might be a diva if . . . You have to always look for
New clothes, new accessories, constantly. *The View* made
Ordinary viewers over into divas. It has to do with the
Presence and the aura and energy. And the January issue
     of *Cosmopolitan*'s
Quiz asked women, "Are you a diva?" Today, divas
Rule like during no other time in pop culture. Yes,
     they've been around
Since the beginning (Remember Eve?). A diva, then, is
     timeless. It's the word
That's tired. The D-word. Do you know one worthy of
     recognition? Let
Us know about them. Write to Divawatch. Rating system:
     Three Tiaras—divalicious.
Viva la diva. La diva loca. Spreading diva-liciousness.
     Thus
Was born a new diva consciousness. Perhaps you're a Gen-
X pop icon. Diva, Diva, on the wall—Or maybe
You believe in the—Deluge of Divas—
Zeitgeist of our times. Who's the fairest of them all?
     Leave it to diva!

By the end of the 1990s, the term "diva" was proliferating across a range of media outlets, and I had decided to devote my entire dissertation to studying what it meant to remember Selena. I interviewed a young woman named Claudia Perez who had auditioned for the role of *Selena* in the Warner Brothers biopic and had reported on it with incisive nuance for an episode of *This American Life*. I learned from Claudia and other fans about the central role that Selena's vibrant afterlife was playing in the lives of so many brown folks like me.

In the summer of 1999 while I was transcribing my research interview notes, *Ms.* magazine's regular opinion column, *Word*, featured a piece titled "Diva" by Holly Morris, former editor of Seal Press and creator of the PBS documentary series *Adventure Divas*. In the show's promotional video, Morris declares, *Women see in other women what they're capable of. They see the diva. I have to admit part of my motivation is wanting to become a diva myself.* As she tells it in her *Ms.* magazine article, on the occasion of her thirtieth birthday, Morris was experiencing corporate burnout and a longing for spiritual awakening and for a return to her feminist principles. She left her office job and began brainstorming her new resolutions, searching for a name for her newfound path: *I rolled the new ethos around in my mouth, feeling for a name—a word around which to hang this emerging philosophy. Forever a fan of four-letter words, I blurted out, "Diva." Diva* \dē-və\ *n: . . . the first person incarnation of feminism's best principles.* So, a decade before diva becomes, for Beyonce, a female version of a hustla, she is first recast as a white feminist version of a hustler: a self-reinventing individual driven by personal passions rather than collective thought and aiming for self- rather than structural transformation. *Diva allowed me to keep my feminist ideals and write my own marching orders. . . . I did push-ups, cranked my Sleater-Kinney albums, tangoed with my fears, skateboarded to work, and jumped out of airplanes.* Look at her leap tall buildings with a single word.

Morris's declaration appeared the year after *Time* magazine published its provocative June 29, 1998 cover story, "Is Feminism Dead?" featuring a lineup of disembodied black-and-white headshots of Susan B. Anthony, Betty Friedan, and Gloria Steinem followed by an in-color headshot of the television character "Ally McBeal." In the accompanying article, "Feminism: It's All About Me," Ginia Bellafante bemoaned feminism's focus on self-obsession rather than societal concerns. Erica Jong, author of the second-wave feminist classic novel *Fear of Flying*, issued a response on July 13, 1998 in an *Observer* article, "Ally McBeal and Time Magazine Can't Keep the Good Women Down," insisting that while the word may have fallen out of fashion, feminism was far from dead. Neither Bellafante nor Jong were wrong. It was the '90s and we were immersed in a culture of celebrity (*For now is the era of the diva*) and the f-word was passé. No wonder Morris needed a new word for this new brand of feminism, for feminism as a brand.

Oh, the journey "diva" took in the closing decade of the twentieth century. Karen Heller had hailed popular diva performers as inaugurators of a new era of female power back in 1992; by the decade's close, Morris concerned herself with the term itself as a conceptual tool for defining the contours of (post)feminist aspiration. A diva is a larger-than-life woman. A diva is a haughty pop star. A diva is an everyday drag queen. A diva is saving the music. A diva is an aspiration. A diva is a self-disciplined (*I did push-ups!*), skateboarding, white girl. A diva is just another dirty word. The d-word is just another word for the f-word. The d-word is a repudiation of the f-word. A diva is the collision of neoliberal and postfeminist forces. And, is it really a surprise given the diva's long-standing and long-derided associations with singularity and accumulation? A diva is a train wreck. Disorienting as a storm of corn husk and silk filling the window frame.

That's how it is with wrecks. Nearly impossible to fully process what's happening in the moment. Sometimes it happens so fast you can't feel anything at first. Sometimes it feels like a slow accumulation of awareness. Sometimes it's a rumbling that brings you to your knees. *A firm terrible hindering.* Sometimes you survive and run-stumble away from the wreckage, but you carry it with you for the rest of your life. Sometimes, like the diva, despite the odds, you endure.

I tried to drown out the noise. Because I also knew that, at least for a colored girl like me, the diva's voice still carried in a register that could, as shange writes, *sing her sighs / sing the song of her possibilities.* I hit play on Lauryn Hill's *Miseducation* CD spinning in the boom box and opened the windows to my Chicago apartment even though they faced the fire station and turned up the volume because a diva's voice was the only sound that could drown out the sirens, the regular blare of all those emergencies. This is how I began merging my growing feminist consciousness with my love of divas. How I began writing my dissertation and eventual book on Selena's enduring legacy, how I began to reckon deeply with praising and mourning and analyzing and safeguarding—by which I mean loving—divas. How I began to learn that the space of grieving a diva was capacious enough for holding the sorrow arising from all the losses that emptied out and filled up our daily lives.

I survived the pileup of personal and political devastation in the 1990s—the deaths of my beloved divas, the neoliberal destruction of state resources, immigration and welfare reform, shiny stiletto-heeled postfeminist slogans—because I followed the voices of Black feminists and Black divas, in particular. Voices that led me and so many other colored girls toward a clearing where our own voices could join together in shriek or in song. Because sometimes in the midst of the wreck your instinct is to reach out for something to hold—a shared dream, a pellet of yellow, a swath of aqua sequins, a rose, a recipe, a bulletproof sense of style, a braid, a ballad, a soaring note. A diva has to hold on to Aretha.

You have to watch all the way to the end to appreciate the diva's enduring power.

You have to keep watching even after it seems the scripted program has ended.

After all the divas have sung their solos to "Save the Music."

After President Clinton hands over his saxophone and after the Black children, on cue, express their thanks. After the camera captures Clive Davis in the audience looking approvingly upon the evening's proceedings.

After Gloria Estefan, in the middle of her set, says, *This diva thing is getting a little out of hand, I think.* After Shania Twain lip-syncs her way through "Man, I Feel Like a Woman" and after Celine Dion pounds her chest to show that, yes, indeed, her heart will go on. After Aretha Franklin lets Mariah Carey join her for what she reveals is an unrehearsed duet on "Chain of Fools." After Gloria and Celine and Shania gather around the piano to harmonize with Carole King as she plays her classic, "You've Got a Friend."

After all the divas line up to sing "(You Make Me Feel Like) A Natural Woman." After Aretha parts the sea of divas like Moses and stands at the center, her microphone the risen staff leading us all to freedom. After she sings over Carole and usurps Celine's turn. After the divas figure out that, really, no matter their skills or their assigned lyrics, they're just there to back her up.

After Aretha's shoulders writhe and her voice runs up and down the scales. After no one can keep up though Carole and Celine earnestly try. After Aretha says, *They're pretty back there aren't they?* and gestures toward a darkened section upstage and goes on to introduce her actual backup singers: *These are my singers, ladies and gentlemen! Mr. Billy Always, Ms. Diane Madison, Ms. Mae Koen.*

After the divas sing the last verse. After Aretha catches the spirit and shimmies and shimmers and shakes across the stage and raises her right hand to God. After her melisma after melisma make you feel like a natural wonder or like you've climbed up the ice-slicked mountain or fallen deep into the riven earth.

After the song is over and she points to her piano man and says, *Take it away.*

After he takes it away.

After she turns to the audience and instructs, *Y'all might as well get ready 'cause we're gonna have church tonight!* After she takes us to church. After she sings out the words *Jesus* and *Higher* over and over and over again.

After the credits start to roll.

After you think the bloom is off the rose.

After Gloria and Carole just finally put down their mics and clap along. After Celine, try as she might to go higher, can only touch the foam of Aretha's wake. After Aretha sings, *Will you help me lift it?* and you want nothing more than to help her lift it or, really, if you're honest, to be the thing she lifts up. After her voice turns to gravel and lava and northern star and heaven's pearly gates flung wide open.

After the veils have been lifted from your eyes and you finally see that a rose is still a rose.

You have to watch until you witness her ascension *Higher!* until you are moved *Higher!* Until you understand how she jumps the rails of the script. How she won't finish by singing a song written by a white girl no matter how gifted she may be and no matter that the song has long ago become her own. How she has to take us back to the source of her Black power. How even as she is directed to save the music she insists on saving our souls. How she remains the Queen of Soul. How she won't be reined in though the credits may roll. How she will only reign.

7

Diva Relations
Celia and La India

Gina is pressing her palm into the small of my back—the slightest gesture—just enough for me to know it's time to break the frame for a turn. We're at the Aragon Ballroom sometime in the late spring of 1995. Chicago winter is long and Selena is dead and we need to move among others who know how to hold the frame or how to break it so you can spin out or get down or lift off and still have a tether to some sense of home. The dance floor here is spacious so I can spin in a wide path, extend my free arm far out. Still, by force of habit I keep my circle tight. As brown girls, we learned long ago how to flair and flaunt in tight quarters.

It's just after midnight, and the opening act—the Dominican salsero, "El Canario"—is still going strong, so I head back to our booth to take a nap before the main act starts. I curl into the cushioned bench, having perfected my dance hall napping skills at countless family weddings as a child. I drift off just long enough for the ice to melt in my drink and awaken to the call: *¡Azúcar!* Celia Cruz launches her set with her signature shout. It's 1 a.m. and the show's just getting started. Celia's 69; I'm 24. I'm the one who needed a nap.

Celia arrives like a meteor, an impossibly bright flare, her impact shaking the earth. Shining in sequins and lamé and salsa dancing across the stage in her famous gravity-defying platform heels. We've all come out for Celia, and she's come out at last, her voice moving us toward morning. We hold the frame. We break it. We are serious about salsa, which is, I suppose, the only way to be.

Salsa has long defied classification and a singular origin story. Most agree that salsa, as a musical genre, emerged in 1960s and '70s New York City. It was a moment electrified by the contact and collaboration among growing numbers of immigrants from Latin America and most especially from across the Caribbean. Music scholar Frances Aparicio defines salsa as *a conjunction of Afro-Cuban music (el son) and rhythms of Puerto Rican bombas and plenas, and of African American jazz instrumentation and structures.* Salsa's Afro-diasporic rhythms keep your center of gravity low as you move across space, and its Spanish-language lyrics keep your mind moving from topics like romantic love to commentaries about social and political conditions like immigration or AIDS or domestic abuse. Rhythmically, lyrically, and kinesthetically, salsa carries within it the traditions of survival and innovation of our people who were subjected to the long durée of plantation slavery and forced migration and countless forms of violence across the Americas. In other words, salsa is quintessentially American music.

When Celia Cruz arrived in New York City in 1961, she had been singing for over a decade with the Cuban band Sonora Matancera. They had left Cuba in 1960 just after the revolution to perform on a year-long contract in Mexico followed by a tour in the United States. Though not her original plan, Celia never returned to Cuba (Fidel Castro had refused

Celia Cruz at the Latin Grammy Awards

her request to return to care for her dying mother in 1962) and
settled into life in exile in New York and eventually New Jer-
sey, where she died in 2003 at age 77. By the time of her passing, she had recorded over seventy albums, including a final
one released the year after her death.

In New York City, Celia encountered and collaborated
with musicians like famed Nuyorican percussionist Tito
Puente and Dominican composer-musician Johnny Pacheco,
who were taking part in creating salsa. Her 1974 album *Celia
y Johnny*, with Pacheco (co-founder of Fania Records, the
label that released and promoted most of the salsa from that
era), and her performance with the Fania All-Stars later that
year in a concert in Zaire, set into full swing her career as a
salsa vocalist.

There's a clip from 1974 that circulates on the internet—
an outtake from the 2009 documentary, *Soul Power*—of Celia
and the Fania All-Stars running a sound check in the empty
stadium in Kinshasa as they rehearse for their festival performance later that evening. Celia is surrounded by men—Johnny
Pacheco, Ray Barretto, Larry Harlow, Hector Lavoe—as they
confer about what song to play. A ribbon of low clouds circles
the sky just above the stadium's highest seats. Celia is dressed
in what I would call Latina diva casual, wearing a bold floral
print dress with a fitted bodice and wide, pointed lapels and
a full A-line skirt that hits just below her knees. She wears
silvery eyeshadow, black eyeliner, fake eyelashes, and strappy
platform heels. Thick turquoise hoops sway from her ears and
soft black curls nimbus her head. Her everyday look.

Celia proposes "Guantanamera" with a shrug, and the
musicians take their places. Pacheco directs the band and then
lifts a flute to his mouth as the piano takes flight. Celia looks
on and then seems to realize suddenly she should join in. She
turns to the camera and says, "Pa'lla!" pointing to the micro-

phone behind her as she saunters over, giving directions to the band along the way, making her mark at exactly the right measure, and singing the opening line, *Guantanamera, guajira Guantanamera*. The flute circles and the rest of the band gallops along, but they can't catch her as she ascends on the second line, a repetition and revision of the first: *Guantanameeeerrrrrrraaaaa, guajira Guantanamera*. Her voice on that one stretched syllable—*meeeerrrrrr*—a thunder clap, a rumble. The plates of the earth shift. And you can't help but fall in.

It's a sound check. And she's singing full-out, which is the only way she knows how. She launches into the first verse and the camera zooms in as she smiles wide, the signature gap between her front teeth a portal, a fault line—the continental divide—and you're falling in all over again. By the time the chorus comes around again she's deep in the earth's core, all the way into the song, her whole body flowing like magma.

It's a sound check and she's already singing the second verse when Jerry Masucci, the other co-founder of Fania Records, taps her on the shoulder, catches her glance, and motions to her to say, "All good, the levels are set, you can stop now" and Pacheco leans in to agree and she never not once not even for half a breath stops singing all the way out. When she sings the chorus for the third time she lifts her right arm into the frame and you notice that she's been casually holding her eyeglasses this whole time. It's a sound check, after all. She finishes the chorus and, glasses still in hand, turns and backsteps her way upstage, salsa dancing with herself as the band plays on. She's a volcano erupting and we're Pompeii. It's two-and-a-half minutes of *I am not playing*. Or, more precisely, of *Look at how seriously I play*. Of *You wanna be startin' something?* Of *When you start something you better see it through. All the way the fuck through. Let me show you how.*

Celia shows us how to show up. Some might say she was, like any diva would be, playing it up for the camera. But

I think she was just showing up for work. Glasses in hand. Singing for a stadium that only looked empty to the untrained eye. She sang and her voice cracked open the ground beneath her. The very ground, it was purported, that was soaked with the blood of prisoners held in the stadium for execution by Zaire's U.S.-backed dictator, Mobutu Sese Seko. Mobutu had raided the country's coffers of millions of dollars to refurbish the soccer stadium—to scrub it clean of the evidence from its previous uses—in preparation for the music festival and the famed "Rumble in the Jungle" fight between Muhammad Ali and George Foreman that followed a few weeks later. But no one could stop Celia's voice from going all the way in, from resounding deeply enough to hold all the bloodshed and all the buried, to hold all of it up if even for only the length of an unfurled syllable.

The sound of her voice on that *meeeerrrrrrr*. That's Celia. The voice synonymous with salsa. A combination of earth and star, the iron heated until it glows and struck until it curves, a warm and deep contralto that melts the boundaries of gender. Rich as molasses but agile as the hand wielding the blade that cuts the cane. A voice whose sonorous tones and dexterous enunciations capture both the toils and virtuosity of Black Cuban labor and the delight in the fruit it bears.

It's hard to overemphasize the significance of Celia's presence as a Black woman, of the sound of her voice searing through the overwhelmingly male-dominated, lighter-skinned realm of salsa. She was outrageously, divinely, resonantly, swaggeringly *Yemayá* and *Ochun con Chango* and *Quimbara* Black in a musical genre that's never been entirely at ease with letting its Afro-diasporic roots show—at least not in the form of Black artists on stage. So she took to the stage—she took the stage—and swathed it in a Blackness only rivaled by the heavens. On the lead single from her fifty-ninth studio album, *La Negra Tiene Tumbao*, released in 2001, the expansive reservoir of Celia's voice holds salsa and reggae and hip hop and son cubano as she declares, *Esta negrita tiene tumba'o / Todos la siguen por su camina'o.* [This Black girl's got swagger / Everyone follows her path.] Her warp-speed lyrical phrasing, her vocal timbre as deep and textured as a ship's hull, her improvisatory shouts invoking Santería gods, her towering wigs in electric hues that made her Black face gleam, and her gravity-defying custom-made shoes—all of it kept her above it all, a dark star in deepest space assuring us we could never ever reach her heights even as we were lifted up by her voice.

I had spent the months before showing up at the Aragon shoving the furniture against the walls to make room to salsa with my girlfriends—Gina, Michelle, Heather, and Regina Jean—across the scuffed wood floors of our apartments. We were in the early years of graduate school, only just learning how to be thinkers and researchers and writers and artists and activists and teachers and girlfriends and grownups. How to

Defying gravity

take on a task that seemed beyond our capacities—a PhD, a
relationship, a heartbreak—and how to carry it through.

We danced.

On weekends after payday we'd bundle up, salsa shoes dan-
gling from our mittened hands, and pile into Heather's van,
which doubled on those nights as a dressing room. Heather
would drive us to the Hot House or Nacional 27 or La Tropi-
cana, or any of the several thriving salsa clubs in town. On the
way, we'd peel off our winter layers and change into our salsa
shoes before running a few haphazardly snow-shoveled blocks
from the dimly lit street where we'd parked, steam rising from
our panting mouths, toward the pulsing warmth of the club.
We knew how to follow and how to lead, how to negotiate
power, so we never had to wait around to be asked to dance.

It was the 1990s, and salsa was experiencing a resurgence
in popularity due, for better or worse, to the widespread com-
mercialization of the genre. Critics often deride the salsa from
this period, generally referred to as *salsa romántica*, for the lack
of musical sophistication and lyrical gravitas that marked salsa
music of the golden era in the 1960s and '70s. They're not
entirely wrong, but their claims usually fail to acknowledge
the feminist interventions in the genre made by salsa artists of
the 1990s like La India and the enduring presence and contributions of Celia. Long-reigning as the Queen of Salsa, Celia
was enjoying renewed popularity following the success of her
contributions to the *Mambo Kings* soundtrack in 1991, the
release of her 1993 Grammy-nominated album *Azúcar Negra*,
and long overdue recognition from President Bill Clinton with
a National Medal of the Arts Award in 1994. She was showing
us how to see things through. For even as salsa and countless
other "Latin" products were being marketed as part of a larger
cultural "Latin Boom," many of us continued to mark out a
hallowed space for ourselves on the rapidly commodifying
dance floor. For us, dancing to Celia and La India was the way

we forged our bonds as women of color in spaces that ceded us little space in which to move.

Celia's longevity created a space for us to coordinate our movements, to move closer to one another at a time when it would have been so easy to believe that success meant standing apart. The exclusionary space of graduate school maintained its closed borders by trying to convince colored girls like us that our numbers were few because we were exceptions to our people, not representative of them, that there was only room for one of us in the tokened spotlight. But our dancing taught us otherwise, reminding us that we belonged to and were long disciplined by a community of exceptional women like Celia and La India.

Celia cleared a path for La India, a Puerto Rican–born, Bronx-bred salsera from our generation who got her start in the Latin freestyle music scene. She was born Linda Viera Caballero in Río Piedras and became known to salsa fans as La India when Eddie Palmieri produced her first salsa album, *Llegó la India via Eddie Palmieri*, in 1992. But it was the release of her now classic 1994 salsa album, *Dicen Que Soy*, that carried her trademark earth-rumbling voice across the world. In the years after, she garnered more number-one salsa hits than any other Latina salsera and became known for her cigar-smoking persona and her public battles with manic depression and with domestic and sexual violence. La India and Celia offered complimentary diva personas: Celia was stalwart, never letting any cracks show; La India let it all hang out. Celia was the chalice; La India was the wine spilling from it. We needed them both because sometimes we danced to keep it together and sometimes we danced to break it all down.

In regular rotation on our multi-disc CD players in those days were songs like Celia's title track from *Azúcar Negra* and La India's feminist salsa anthem, "Ese Hombre," a hit song from *Dicen Que Soy*. In Celia's song we heard Black diasporic blood memory—*mi sangre es azúcar negra* [my blood is black sugar]—and an insistence that salsa would carry us through the everyday and the holy days—proclaiming herself as both street and carnival. Her song reminded us that the rhythms to which we moved were drawn from the source of our people's long laboring and were, as well, its exalted product—*soy la caña y el café* [I am the cane and the coffee]. In La India's song, we rejoiced in her rueful subversion of the *romántica* trope and structure of *salsa romántica*. Her lyrics begin by beckoning us to look upon a man who appears so gallant, and then just as the horns blare and your body launches into its first sequence of moves, she turns generic convention on its head with the chorus that describes him as *un gran necio . . . un payaso* vanidoso . . . *Que no tiene corazón* [a great fool . . . a vain clown . . . who has no heart].

It's not just La India's words in "Ese Hombre" but her voice that grabs ahold of me every time. How it offers up its crystal chalice—so exquisite, so pristine—filled to the brim with blood, how it hurls itself across the room and shatters against the walls built to enclose it. In the first verse and chorus, La India's clear soprano scales a glass staircase, picking up speed, taking two steps at once by the time she gets to the end of the second verse. But when the chorus returns for its second round, she lowers her voice to a deep growl on words like *caprichoso* [capricious] and *cariñoso* [affectionate], smashing all those fairy-tale steps promising ascendance. Perhaps what I love best, though, is when she takes the clawed paw of her voice and swats and swats at the seemingly anodyne conjunctions like *que* [that/which/who] and *como* [as/like] throughout the song as if reminding us that no place is safe from betrayal and from the revenge we enact against it.

I'm a feminist, La India will declare in an interview some years later, *It's about survival. It's about working hard and giving your heart and soul, and being professional. And if that makes you*

*obnoxious, arrogant, if that makes you a snob or a bitch—and that's
what they call me—well, then let me be a bitch, then.* I prefer to call
her, reverentially, a diva.

We moved the couch. We rolled up the rug. We soaked
our outfits with sweat—our own and each other's—holding on
so closely. We danced to the voices of La India and Celia. We
showed up that night at the Aragon because, sure, we wanted
to be in the presence of a living legend, to bow—and turn and
glide and shuffle and spin—before the Queen. But, mostly, we
came because we wanted to dance to rhythms that resonated
with our current lives. For us, Celia was not just an emblem
of salsa's grand past but a relevant and vibrant force that continued to charge its present and shape its future. Celia was
of her time and capable of transcending it. She continually
reinvented herself while maintaining an immutable sense of
her signature divinity. Which is to say she was a diva. Celia
opened her mouth, the band lifted their horns, and we found
ourselves and each other on the dance floor.

Some of us danced "on the 1" (*step-step-step-pause*); others
"on the 2" (*pause-step-step-step*). To those who were perhaps
more sophisticated, or maybe just more rigid, than we were at
the time, what you danced on or where you took the pause in
salsa was often regarded as a defining measure of authenticity.
The pause, as dance scholar Cindy Garcia observes, *is the most
crucial component of the dance—potentially sensual and volatile.*
Maybe because we were naïve or maybe because we knew we'd
never measure up or maybe because of our developing feminist
consciousness, we took turns taking the lead without judgment
about when our partner took her pause. Whether on the one
or on the two, for us it all added up to a sum greater than our
individual parts. To learn how to salsa was to learn about your
relationship to time, about how to measure it and move to it
and dwell in its pauses. We suspended ourselves in the space of
the pause that salsa granted us. Sometimes we held it in a state

of reflection. Other times as a site of daring improvisation. We held the pause. We held each other in secure and supple frames. We were held by a diva's voice.

Salsa dancing demands that your body sustains opposing tensions. You keep a low center of gravity, moving the lower half of your body fluidly forward and back and side to side and sometimes at an angle and with an occasional flared kick while your upper body remains placid, a stilled frame with an occasional flared arm. And atop this seemingly irresolvable paradox, your face is doing something altogether different. Gina and I spent more than a small amount of time sharing our theories about the "salsa face"—that mask of ennui, of IDGAF, of opacity, even. The salsa face says down below I may be dancing as fast as I can, but up above, at this height, I'll never betray the confidences my body keeps. The salsa face says I could do this all night and not break a sweat and you could watch me all night and never really know me or locate the source of my weakness or my power.

I've tried to find photos of us dancing together to Celia or La India to offer a record of our salsa faces, but in those days we were usually all on the dance floor at once and, anyway, this was in the time before smart phones with cameras. I did manage to retrieve one photo of Gina and me salsa dancing to "Ese Hombre" as we often did at house parties, though we were moving too fast for the camera to capture our faces. What the photograph does record clearly is our secure frame as we hold onto one another. I am leading—I can tell from the position of our arms—and Gina's left hand is perfectly poised atop my right shoulder. We are dancing in someone's apartment framed in the doorway between two rooms. I can tell it is winter because hanging on the wall above us is a Christmas decoration of a bear with a Santa hat atop the word "JOY." A caption, perhaps. More likely, a mile marker La India is helping us reach.

Holding the frame

La rumba me está llamando [The rumba is calling me], Celia sings in the opening lyrics of her signature 1974 hit, "Quimbara," and we answered the call. We moved the coffee table, we shared the lead, we felt for the pause, we donned our salsa faces, we tried and tried to keep up with Celia's vocal gymnastics and the song's exhilarating tempo. Salsa dancing was how we were learning to keep up with each other, to keep each other close. How we were coming to know who we were in relation to one another. And dancing to "Quimbara," with its impossibly fast rhythms and tumbling lyrics, not only offered us a source of deeply embodied pleasure but trained us to out-maneuver and outspeak and outrun any foes who sought to slow us down. *Divas required other women as models, mentors, and admirers,* Wayne Koestenbaum writes. *Without the example of other forthright, independent women, how could a diva imagine and pursue this vocation in which subservience to men seemed to play no part?*

The year after her concert at the Aragon, Celia will record a duet with La India called "La Voz de la Experiencia." The song, written by La India, is at once an homage to Celia as *La Reina de La Salsa* and an enactment of the crowning of La India, *La Princesa de La Salsa*, as the successor to the throne. The duet moves from *batá* drumming to high brass, from sec-ular *salsa romántica* arrangements to invocations of the Yoruba deity Yemayá. Throughout, the women take turns admiring one another, and their declarations act as well as an acknowl-edgment of the larger cultural and national influences each woman brings to the genre as an Afro-Cuban and a New York City–raised Puerto Rican. Both musically and lyrically, the song acknowledges and embodies the diasporic range of salsa's traditions rather than succumbing to the nationalist tenden-cies that have framed the debates about salsa's origins. It's no surprise that it took two women singing together in a predom-inantly masculine genre for this declaration to happen.

On the surface, the duet is framed as a lesson in diva mentorship, with La India seeking counsel and Celia, as the anointed "voice of experience," imparting her wisdom about how to make it as a woman in the business, and insisting above all: *Tienes que estar en control . . . Ten control control* [You've got to be in control . . . Have control, control]. Admittedly, the advice is, at best, aphoristic, but for me, that's not where the song's power lies. The song's force, its summoning of con-trol, comes through in the sound of two women unabash-

edly worshipping one another in a highly exclusionary space
that would otherwise have them competing for the one token
"girl" spotlight.

It's a song they sang together live on a number of occasions,
most notably, perhaps, during Celia's televised concert for
PBS, "Celia Cruz and Friends: A Night of Salsa," which took
place in Hartford, Connecticut, on May 12, 1999, and aired on
PBS on December 7th of that year. By the time La India joins
Celia onstage for their duet, the audience is already dancing in
the crowded aisles and Celia has changed her costume from a
rumba-style ruffled polka-dot dress to a dazzlingly sequined
floor-length outfit (with matching headpiece, of course) composed of multicolored, diamond-shaped geometric prints.

The winter that their duet airs, I am living with Regina Jean
and we've just signed up for birthing classes at a nearby hospi-
tal to train me as her birth partner as she prepares to give birth
the following spring. We're still moving the furniture aside for
dancing. I have my salsa shoes re-soled. I haven't finished my
dissertation. But I have, at least, mastered the salsa kick that
seasoned dancers sometimes make before leaning into a back-
step. A gesture of flare and confidence and experience.

At the end of their duet performance in 1999, La India falls
to her knees at Celia's feet in a grand diva successor act of
worship and gratitude. Celia immediately responds matter-of-
factly with the command, *¡Levántate! ¡Levántate!* Get up, she
instructs. And then she helps La India to her feet. It's time to
rise, she is saying with this gesture. There's work to be done.
New movements to learn and to join. *Tienes que estar en control.*
Ten control control.

In the months after Celia and La India's duet, Heather,
Michelle, and I will let the music play while we hold Regina
Jean's back and legs as she gives birth to her daughter. We'll
finish our dissertations. We'll move away. We'll launch our
careers in departments and institutions that are mostly white

and male. Years will pass. Celia will die. So many salsa clubs
will shutter. My hip will ache.

I'll hang on to my salsa shoes, re-heeled and polished
countless times, though over the years I'll move the furniture
only when I'm packing up to move apartments. I will struggle
to see things through. I'll move into a new place. And another.
In each one, I'll hang a framed excerpt from a poem by Yehuda
Amichai given to me by a poet I once knew back in Chicago:

In the place where you love,
all the furniture has to be cleared out from the room

all the trees, all the mountains, all the oceans.
The world is too narrow.

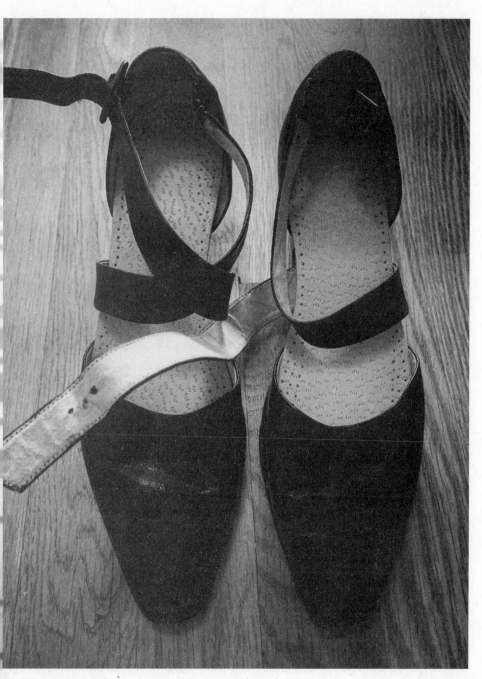

Re-soled and polished

8

Diva Girls
Venus and Serena

Summertime and the winning is easy. At least for Venus. The sun overtakes the clouds above as she easily defeats her opponent, Rossana de los Ríos, taking the first set in six straight games and the match in just over an hour. It's the second round of the 2008 US Open Tennis Tournament, and I'm cheering for Venus from the stands of Arthur Ashe Stadium with my husband Frank. After the match, we roam the grounds, delightedly catching a glimpse of Venus's sister Serena, practicing before her match later that evening, which she will win in just 58 minutes. Frank and I are in the early years of our marriage and have discovered that one of our love languages is watching tennis, or, more precisely, watching Venus and Serena Williams dominate and transform the tennis world. These are our salad days of assistant professor salaries and towering student loan debt and a new mortgage, but we've splurged on two day tickets to the tournament, the more expensive night tickets still out of our price range. Venus is fresh off her Wimbledon Women's Singles Championship, having defeated Serena in the finals match the month before. I'm pregnant with my daughter and about to embark on a sabbatical. So much seems possible. *One of these mornings / You're gonna rise up singing.*

Six days later, Venus and Serena return to Arthur Ashe Stadium for the Women's Quarterfinals, playing one another in what will be hailed by *Tennis* magazine as the best women's singles match in any tournament that year. It's the fourth time they will meet at the US Open (Venus having won two of the three previous matches) and the seventeenth time they will play each other in a tournament (each securing eight previous wins). Venus arrives on the court in a sleek black tennis dress and matching visor from her fashion label, EleVen, that she had launched the year before. Serena is wearing a red dress and headband, both marked by the Nike swoosh. Serena had signed a $40 million endorsement deal with Nike in 2003, and in the years to come their partnership will become so profitable for the company that Nike will name their largest office building after her and invite her to collaborate on its interior design.

Frank and I watch the match on television, cheering for both sisters, though as elder siblings ourselves, we have a soft spot for Venus. Serena trails for the first several games but goes on to win the set in a hard-fought tiebreak. Venus triumphs for the first half of the second set but Serena perseveres, gradually overtaking her older sister and forcing another tiebreak in a display of exhilarating play from both sisters. Venus delivers a blistering 125-mile-an-hour serve. Serena leaps cross-court and back again to return what seem like impossible shots. Their astonishing rally for Venus's fifth point in the second-set tiebreak prompts an uproarious standing ovation. Serena goes on to win the two-hour-and-twenty-five-minute-long match, the longest on record in any of their matchups. There's a moment near the end of the match captured in slow-motion instant replay when Serena runs at the net, explodes from a split step, and lifts off the ground, her left hand rising behind her while her right holds the racket low and angled to execute a perfect backhand. She defies gravity. *One of these mornings . . . You're gonna spread your wings / And take to the sky.*

Their matchup in the quarterfinal round is unusual for the Williams sisters, the early meetup resulting largely from their lower rankings due to decreased participation in qualifying tournaments in the preceding year. The last time they had met in the US Open was in 2002, when Serena beat Venus in the final round while wearing a gleaming and controversial black catsuit designed by Bonnie Dominguez, a senior designer at Puma (Serena's previous sponsor), and inspired by Eartha Kitt's iconic portrayal of Catwoman. Black femme superhero legacy for sure. But in the years since 2003, both sisters had nursed various injuries and pursued other passions that included attending design school, launching a fashion line, taking up Billie Jean King's fight for equal pay for women players, and starring in a reality television series, *Venus and Serena: For Real*, that aired for one season in 2005. The pilot episode launched with the sisters volleying the lines: *People often ask us what we think about during a match. We think about winning. But we also worry about losing. We think about family. We think about friends. . . . And fashion. And design. And the future. Yeah, we're tennis players. But we're a whole lot more.* In response, the tennis establishment and sponsors expressed dismay and doubts about their ability to make a comeback; Chris Evert published an "Open Letter to Serena" in the May 2006 issue of *Tennis* bemoaning her lack of commitment to the game.

But here they are defying the naysayers yet again in 2008. Summertime and the winning is easy. At least for Serena. Landing aces. Covering the baseline. Returning all those shots. After Serena beats Venus in the quarterfinals, she sails through the semifinal round and triumphs in the finals, reclaiming her number 1 ranking at the US Open for the first time in five years while Venus and her mother and father cheer from the stands. She doesn't lose a single set during the entire tournament. The following year Serena will win the Women's Singles Championship at the Australian Open and at Wimbledon (where she'll play Venus again in the finals match) and in between these victories, I'll give birth to my daughter. Another brown girl with so much promise arriving in the world. *Hush, little baby,* I hum with hope and dread and fierce resolve, *Ain't nothing can harm you / With daddy and mama / Standing by.*

The spring of 2009 passes in a haze of diaper changes and nightly feedings. I channel-surf through the morning's blue hour, scrolling past commercials for *Hannah Montana* and the Barbie Gymnastics Divas dolls as the baby cries in my arms. *Hannah Montana,* in its third season on the Disney Channel that spring, is all the rage and has spawned the feature-length film *Hannah Montana: The Movie* that premieres to great commercial success in April 2009, a week before my daughter is born. The show and the film feature the diva girl–pop star Miley Cyrus, who brings her girl diva aura to the role of Miley Stewart, an ordinary brown-haired girl by day who secretly performs as the platinum-haired diva girl superstar Hannah Montana by stage-light-dazzled night. Apparently, divas are now bedazzled white girls and white girls are undercover divas who remain loyal to their ordinary calling. The gleam sears my sight. I click the remote and tune in to reruns of *Girlfriends* as I try to rock the baby back to sleep.

I'm in search of a bedtime story to tell my brown girl. Another kind of story about girls who transform themselves into virtuosic and shimmering divas. Girls whose glint is more Eartha Kitt's catsuit than Hannah Montana's highlights. *Once upon a time,* I begin, *there was a girl, and the girl had a sister. The sisters each possessed special powers as most girls who looked like them—dark velvety skin, braided and beaded hair, gold hoops swaying from their ears—usually developed to survive in their hostile kingdom. They were neither queens nor princesses though they held countless titles and though, as legend has it, they came from a people who could fly. Together they reigned, a pair of glistening verbs in a court of pale-faced nouns, neither ever falling prey to the lie that one should hide one's light under a bushel for the other to shine, and in this way they rose like hands at a revival, like geyser-spray from a summer-sidewalk hydrant, like rockets breaking past the cloud-thudded sky.*

My girl still won't be soothed. She's an Aries, after all, so isn't satisfied with the allegorical or the hagiographical. She wants a more straightforward story. So I tell her how lucky she is to come into the world after Venus and Serena. I emphasize how because of this it may be difficult for her to fully comprehend what the realm of professional tennis was like before them, so profound has been their collective impact on the sport. I tell her stories of how they began training on public courts in their Compton neighborhood as children instead of in exclusive private clubs. How they were coached early on by their parents—Richard and Oracene Williams—rather than in elite training centers for aspiring pros. How they were as supportive as they were competitive with one another in a sport known for its bratty singularity. How they brought an unprecedented level of athleticism and finesse and power to women's tennis. How they showcased their own beaded and jeweled and self-designed Black style in a realm known for its austere white aesthetic. How they dominated the sport after foregoing the junior tournament circuit in favor of finishing high school and then fashion school and getting straight As along the way.

My girl is quieted now, her dark eyes focused and curious. So, I charge toward my story's climax, telling her how, above all—at least for Black and brown girls like us—what was most powerful about the Williams sisters' impact is that they accomplished all of these remarkable feats without apology. How, from the very beginning of their careers, they refused

to portray the humble Black athlete performing genteel gratitude toward the white sports establishment who "let them"
play. I give a short history lesson on this well-known role in
professional sports: the breakthrough, singular, Black figure
who is endeared to the hearts of white players and fans for the
ability to excel without displays of pride and to endure the regular assault of racist indignities heaped upon them with a stoic
grace and a sense of noble diminishment lest their greatness be
too overwhelming a threat. A role that surely took its toll on
the lives of integration pioneers like Jackie Robinson. I tell her
how the Williams sisters tore up the pages of that script. How
they started doing it while they were still girls.

My girl looks up at me quizzically, as if she knows I'm not
telling the whole story. She's wide awake, and it's nowhere near
dawn. She wants details. Not only the glory but the gore. My
brown girl needs to be ready for this world. So, I settle in for a
long night. I've got to start at the beginning, at least the beginning of the century into which she was born. The gory details.
I speak to her in the dark.

On September 3, 2001, during that year's US Open Tennis
Tournament, *Time* published a cover story featuring photos
of Venus and Serena Williams split by the headline: *The Sisters vs. The World.* Below the photos, a subheading proclaimed,
*Taunts! Tantrums! Talent! Why the women, led by Venus and Ser-
ena, are pushing men off center court.* The accompanying article, "The Power Game" by Joel Stein, chronicles—with equal
parts delight and dismay—the rising popularity, new forms of
athleticism, and fierce competitiveness of a new generation of
young women players. For the first time in the sport's history,
the article notes, television ratings for women's tennis were
surpassing men's matches, attendance for women's games was
at an all-time high, *Forbes* Celebrity 100 list included five young

Diva Girl Mad Libs® Erasure Poem: A History Lesson

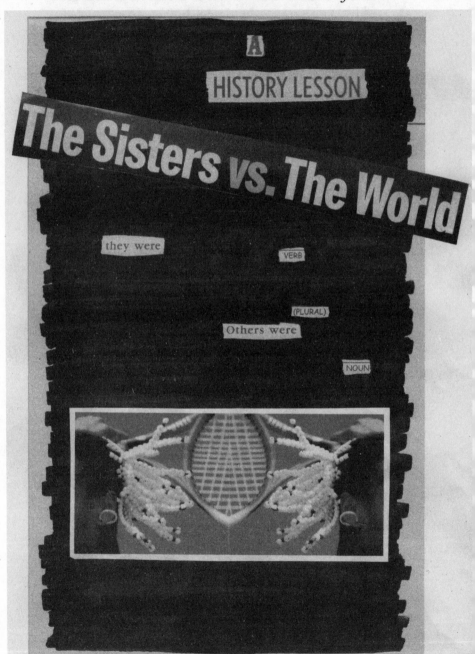

women tennis players (and no male tennis pros) among its ranks, and little girls everywhere were *begging for new rackets.*

For Stein, the Williams sisters (*admired, despised, and certainly controversial*) are both exemplars and exceptions, at once the targets of racist accusations of arrogance and the very paragons of haughtiness among this rising cadre of apparently catty and bratty young women tennis players. *Try to get the women to pose for a magazine cover en masse and you wonder how VH1 pulls off that diva show every year.* The article showcases sidebar statistics of top-ranked players alongside depictions of supposed catfights between them, graphs depicting the historic pay gap between men and women players on the opposing page of a side-eyed anecdote about Venus's and Serena's endorsement deals, assertions of a generalized climate of mean girl competitiveness on the same page as the bold pullout quote from number-one-ranked 20-year-old Swiss player Martina Hingis: *Many times [the Williams sisters] get sponsors because they are black. And they have lots of advantages because they can always say, "It's racism."* The article simultaneously acknowledges the racism that framed the Williams sisters' success and expresses an ambivalence about their rise, and in doing so acutely registers the threat that the sisters' unmatched excellence and approach to tennis posed to the historically white norms of the women's game.

People criticize me for being arrogant, Venus is quoted as saying in the article, *Maybe because I'm a little smarter than the others. Maybe it's because when they ask me a silly question, I refuse to answer it and make myself look foolish.* The sisters' mutually supported self-possession was illegible to those seeking assurance by the presence and legacy of the "grateful Black athlete." Television announcers, sports commentators, spectators, and other tennis pros like Martina Hingis regularly derided them as haughty and unfeminine and aloof and playing the "race card" and just not friendly enough to their fellow players. At the 1997 US Open when the sisters were 17 and 15 years old, Chris Evert chattered disparagingly, *Some of the players have been critical of Venus and the close relationship with her sister, Serena: that they've closed off the rest of the world.* Her sentiment is echoed in *Time*'s cover headline. How dare they be close and protective of each other as sisters in "the world" that shows them so much antagonism! Surely it's them and not "the world" that's the problem!

The awe and alarm expressed by Stein in "The Power Game" echoed a larger obsession with girls and girlhood that pervaded popular culture at the turn of the twenty-first century. It was a moment marked by a shift from the promotion of "girl power" in the 1990s to an era where girls weren't just encouraged but expected to fully embody neoliberal ideals of self-as-marketable-brand. Girl Power had emerged in the 1990s as a commodified version of the anti-establishment "riot grrrl" movement arising from punk and girl-created 'zine culture. As a marketing slogan, Girl Power emphasized individual rather than collective power and encouraged girls to be confident, athletic, independent, consumerist forces to be reckoned with. Girl Power insisted that structures like racism or sexism or homophobia were increasingly inconsequential because girls needed only to rely on hard work and rigorous self-management to achieve anything they wanted. *You go, girls,* Girl Power proclaimed, appropriating the language and attitudes of girls and women of color without accounting for them fully in its assertions of power. You go, girls! Well, at least some of you girls!

By the dawn of the twenty-first century, this idea of girlhood became supersized into a new form: the diva girl. She seemed suddenly to be everywhere—in toddler toys and teen STEM camps, in tween-girl sitcoms and beauty advice columns, in clothing lines and charity campaigns. There was a new girl in town: the Diva Girl of the 2000s replaced and refined "Girl Power" of the 1990s. From *Diva Girl Mad Libs* (topics include "Girl Band" and "Girl Scouts") to *Rescue Divas Camp* (middle-school girls receive EMT training and certification!), from Disney pop star–divas (Miley! Britney! Jessica! Christina!) to disparaging news articles ("I've Had Enough of Diva Girl Groups"!), girls were hailed—with adulation and admonishment—as divas or at least as aspiring to diva status. By 2009, in the month before my daughter was born, *Newsweek* published an article by Jessica Bennett that asked with alarm, "Are We Turning Tweens into 'Generation Diva?'" (The answer was a woeful yes). Bennett bemoaned the increasing *diva-ization* of tweens, measured in large part by young girls' troubling investments in the beauty industry, with eight-to-twelve-year-old girls spending upwards of $40 million dollars a month on beauty products. *Today's girls are getting caught up in the beauty maintenance game at ages when they should be learning how to read.*

The first decade of the new century, as feminist media scholars like Sarah Projansky and Mary Celeste Kearney have chronicled, brought with it increased public preoccupation with girls expressed as both celebration and concern for them as model consumers and shimmering celebrities. Projansky refers to this as an era of "spectacular girls" in which a wide range of media outlets and cultural products invited us to regard girls as spectacles—some fabulous, others scandalous, and still others scandalous because they were so fabulous. And it wasn't just that girls were spectacular; they sparkled. Kearney calls it girlhood's "sparklefication"—through glitter, sequins, bling, fairy dust, Disney-animated lighting effects, and other bedazzlements.

"Girl" as sparkly, spectacular, scandalous, self-managed, shopaholic celebrity. In other words, a mass-produced diva. In the twenty-first century, divas had become girls and girls had become divas. Diva Girl emerged as the latest way to talk

about and worry over and market and constrain girlhood in
the guise of a celebratory spotlight on the accessory-laden,
camera-ready, glitter-gilded performing girl. Indeed, one of
the most popular storylines in the unprecedented number of
films, television shows, and musical plays that showcased girl
protagonists during these years featured girls as aspiring or
established performers. From the Disney films *Cheetah Girls*
(2003) and *Camp Rock* (2008), to Broadway's *Wicked* (2003) and
Nickelodeon's *Victorious* (2010), girls were suddenly dreaming about or disciplining themselves or simply destined to be
divas. This marked a shift from the depictions of girls in film
and television that prevailed in the 1990s: whereas yesterday's
erstwhile ordinary girls were secretly superheroes (think *Buffy
the Vampire Slayer*), girls of the new century were often portrayed as secretly superstars (think *Hannah Montana*). Diva
superstardom became the new girl superpower.

The same year as the *Time* article about the dominance of
girl tennis stars, Mattel released the "Gone Platinum" Barbie, the latest in its Collector's Edition Barbie series and the
first of three "Barbie Diva Collection" dolls that would hit the
shelves over the next year. The Platinum Diva Barbie, as her
name suggests, was sold in a shimmering, silvery box and was
positioned against a glittery background. A description on the
back of the box praised her attributes and her attitude, charac-
terizing her as a mega-superstar, a pop princess, and *the perfect
goddess for today*. Platinum Diva Barbie's long, straight, blonde
hair flows down past her hips; her eyes and lips are shaded with
sparkly platinum hues. She wears a shimmering floor-length,
backless halter gown with a train that cascades behind her, silvery earrings that extend down to her shoulders, sheer white
gloves speckled with silver glitter, and a voluminous white
feather boa atop it all. Packaged for aspiring girl divas, she's a
searing platinum fantasy of white glamour. Looking at her is
like looking into a strobe light.

Platinum Diva Barbie was just one of the diva-themed dolls Mattel released at the turn of the twenty-first century. The "Diva Starz Dolls" had hit the shelves in 2000 and were known for their ability (thanks to metal contacts on their backs) to recognize and comment on the outfits they were wearing. *Do you think it makes my eyes look bluer?* one doll asks upon being dressed. McDonald's featured the Diva Starz dolls in their Happy Meals in 2001, promoting this limited-time offer in a television commercial that zoomed in on three white girls carrying their Happy Meals like handbags as they walk through a throng of paparazzi. Close-ups of each girl playing with the dolls follow, including a shot of a girl using one of the dolls as a brush to smooth her own long, silky hair behind her ears. Narrating these scenes, which are pulsing with camera-flash effects and the sounds of clicking shutters, a sassy young woman's voice says, *Hey, looking too good can be hard on a girl. But now that there's one Diva Starz doll or Div-Accessory in every Happy Meal . . . divas everywhere are learning to deal with it.* The commercial ends with a close-up on one of the shiny, happy girls holding one of her shiny, happy dolls. The diva girl speaks directly into the camera—*No pictures, please!*—as she poses and smiles for the shot.

It takes me dozens of views, but when I look closely enough, when I stop and rewind the commercial and then pause on a quick jump cut of one of the crowded paparazzi scenes, I can see the body of a Black girl, tight curls piled atop her head, briefly enter the frame. The cut happens so quickly that her whole body never makes it all the way into the shot. But she's there. She's been there all along. In the opening scene, she was obscured, positioned behind the flank of white girls, looking away from the camera toward another white girl with a camera who is photographing them. It's easy to miss her at first, but when I slow down and look again, I can see her red skirt and white top splattered with red stars, her small hoop

Serena and Venus gleaming amidst the blinding flashes

earring hugging her delicate brown ear, her hand wrapped
around a straw-topped cup printed with Ronald McDonald's
face. And then, near the end, just before the screen flashes
white with the sound of a camera shutter closing, before the
smiling, sun-drenched closing shot, there she is again, skirt-
ing the edge. Half her body cut out of the frame. She's laughing, her mouth open wide enough to see her teeth as she turns
toward the white divas who fill the frame. It's the moment
in the ad when the voice-over is saying, *divas everywhere are
learning to deal with it.* There she is. Brown face gleaming just

before the screen snow-blanks. She appears amidst all these blinding flashes.

The same year that McDonald's launched its Diva Starz Happy Meal campaign, 19-year-old Serena defeated the favored number-two-ranked Lindsay Davenport 6–1, 6–2 in the Women's Quarterfinals at the Indian Wells Masters tennis tournament. Later that day, 20-year-old Venus sailed to a 6–0, 6–3 straight-set victory over 19-year-old Elena Dementieva. Their wins set Venus and Serena up to meet in a much-anticipated semifinals round. The sisters had entered the tournament having secured eleven Grand Slam singles and doubles titles between them. Serena had won the Indian Wells Masters and US Open championships in 1999 in all of her beaded, 17-year-old glory. The following summer, Venus won the 2000 Wimbledon and US Open championships as well as gold medals in women's singles and doubles (with Serena, of course) at the 2000 Olympics in Sydney. They had come to play.

During the press conference following her defeat to Venus in the quarterfinals, in response to a question about who she thought might win the upcoming semifinals match between Venus and Serena, Dementieva said, *I don't know what Rich-ard [Williams] thinks about it. I think he will decide who's going to win tomorrow.* Later that week, the tabloid paper *National Enquirer* hit the stands with a cover story accusing the family of match-fixing during the sisters' meetup in the Wimbledon Women's Finals Championship the previous year: *Wimbledon Fixed? The Shocking Story—Venus and Serena Williams' Family Member Charges: Dad Ordered Serena To Lose—Tennis Scandal Rocks Family's $160 Million Empire.* How dare these Black sisters be champions on the basis of their own individual and collective excellence! How dare they support one another as fiercely as they competed! How dare they earn enough to secure their family's fortunes! How dare there be two of them when there had only ever been room in the frame—and barely—for one!

At the checkout stands alongside the *National Enquirer* that spring and summer, *Seventeen* magazine featured ads for the latest line of Head Wear hair gel—*Boost your ego with Disco Diva™ Thickening Gel*—and a call for models sponsored by the magazine and PacSun sportswear seeking to *grant one lucky girl her wish to become a Surf Diva at one of Southern California's premiere surf camps*. On the shelf in the toy department at the big-box stores selling these magazines, aspiring diva girls could shop for sparkly tennis rackets and the "Dance Diva Home Recording Studio." The iridescent lavender machine, aimed at girls ages eight and up, featured two microphones (one for a friend!), a cassette tape with karaoke versions of some of the latest teen pop diva hits, and a dual cassette deck that allowed girls to play their favorite songs while recording their own voices as they sang along. The product description on the side of the box promised to bring out everyday girls' inner divas through its *awesome echo effects*, *instant applause button*, and other sparkling features. Confidently ride the waves (or tame them!) and find your voice as a diva girl! We promise instant applause upon your arrival!

The morning of the semifinals match at Indian Wells on March 15, 2001, Venus told the tour trainer that her knee was in pain and that she didn't think she was going to be able to play in the match later that day. Instead of immediately consulting with the tournament director per protocol, the trainer dragged her feet, insisting that Venus hold off on making a final decision. The match was sold out. Sponsors were secured. Venus confirmed with the trainer that she would not be able to play. More delays. At last, four minutes before the match, once the sold-out crowd was already in their seats, tournament officials announced over the loudspeakers that Venus had withdrawn. Serena would advance to the finals by default.

The crowd erupted with boos.

Tournament officials did not quiet the crowd. Nor did they confirm that Venus was legitimately hurt or that she had begun notifying them hours before the match. In a press conference after the announcement of the scratched match, Serena said, *I don't know why everyone is blaming Venus. She told them as soon as she arrived that she couldn't play. Ask the trainer. She'll tell you.* Nobody asked the trainer.

Rumors immediately began circulating that Richard Williams had fixed the match, that the sisters had colluded with him so that Serena could have a chance at the championship. After a day of silence, WTA Tour CEO Bart McGuire issued a statement on March 16th: *The tour is aware of the assertions being circulated regarding Venus and Serena Williams' head-to-head matches. We have seen no evidence to support those assertions, and both players have denied them.* Still, media outlets across the country continued to publish articles that stoked the rumors.

When Serena Williams walked on the court for the Women's Finals on Saturday, March 17th under the glaring desert sun, she looked like a spectacular teenage girl in her pink Puma jumpsuit, tennis visor, heart-shaped pendant necklace, pink barrettes, and two long braids tied at the top of her head.

The crowd of 15,940 erupted with boos. Thousands of boos.

This was shocking, as tennis spectators were traditionally known for their WASP-y displays of restraint, of polite applause and compliant silence at all the right times. Years later Serena, in her 2009 autobiography, *Queen of the Court*, will recall, *It wasn't coming from just one section. It was like the whole crowd got together and decided to boo all at once. The ugliness was just raining down on me, hard.* When her opponent, Kim Clijsters, a 17-year-old blonde-haired Belgian, followed Serena's entrance, the crowd cheered raucously. *Instant Applause Button!* A few minutes later, as Venus and Richard Williams descended the 50 steps toward their seats in the players' box, the crowd resumed their booing. An article in the *New York Times* would later describe how in this moment *the stadium was filled with the eerie howl found in haunted houses.* Fifty steps of booing.

The stunned telecasters, Simon Reed and Jo Durie, were aghast. *It's an amazing sound here. A crescendo of boos for Serena Williams,* Reed remarked, *An American crowd booing an American family. And you have to say that it does smack of a little bit of racism.* After a beat, Durie responded, *Well, I'm just speechless. I've never heard this before. Ever.* The camera followed Venus and Richard down all 50 steps. Just before taking his seat, Richard faced the court and defiantly raised his fist. He would later tell *USA Today* that upon their descent, *people kept calling me "n*****." One guy said, "I wish it was '75; we'd skin you alive."* Venus and Richard sat in this crowd.

The spectators quieted for Clijsters's introduction and then gave her a standing ovation; upon Serena's introduction, their booing and jeering resumed. *I looked up and all I could see was a sea of rich people—mostly older, mostly white—standing and booing lustily like some kind of genteel lynch mob. . . . There was no mistaking that all of this was meant for me. I heard the word n***** a couple times, and I knew.* When Serena missed her first serve of the match, the crowd cheered viciously; when she double-faulted on her second serve, they roared in ecstatic delirium. When Serena hit a forehand into the net to lose the second game of the first set, the crowd erupted in cheers once again, prompting an exasperated Simon Reed to say, *I don't like the atmosphere at all. I do think it smacks of a certain amount of racism by a certain proportion in the crowd, and that is distasteful.* When Clijsters won the first set 6–4, the crowd rose for another standing ovation.

During the changeover following the third game of the second set, Serena, down 2–1, sat in her seat and covered her head with her towel to hide her tears and to shield herself from the venomous taunts. *I didn't think I had it in me to keep going. The booing was just wearing me out.* She talked to herself and to her god. She thought about her dad and her sister. She remembered Althea Gibson, the first Black American player to win a Grand Slam tennis championship amidst an onslaught of racist indignities in the amateur era when it was not possible to earn a living from playing a sport in which she excelled. Serena got back up. *In my head it was no longer a battle between me and Kim Clijsters. Now it was between me and this hateful crowd.* She came from behind to win the second set 6–4 as the crowd booed on.

Just before the third set, the quality of light shifted as the sun began to set. Serena removed her visor. She no longer squinted into the blinding light. As the girls played through the games in the final set, shadows stretched across the court, cutting the glare. It's in this spreading shadow that Serena took control of the match, winning the last set decisively 6–2. When she walked over to hug her father and sister after her win—a customary post-win gesture—the crowd erupted with boos once more. *Nobody would have booed some blond, blue-eyed girl. And nobody would have shouted down her father with cries of, "Go back to Compton, n*****!"*

In the press conference following her win, Serena reminded everyone, *How many people do you know go out there and jeer a 19-year-old? Come on, I'm just a kid.* In her autobiography published eight years later, she continued to offer this reminder that she was a *girl* when the crowd unleashed their vitriol at her at Indian Wells. Her insistence recalls the famed 1995 interview (recreated in the biopic, *King Richard*) between ABC news correspondent John McKenzie and a self-assured, 14-year-old Venus, resplendent in her beaded braids and warm smile. McKenzie notes with surprise Venus's calm confidence; Venus responds, *I'm very confident.* McKenzie pushes, *You say it so easily. Why?* Venus pauses and then says, *Because I believe it*, as Richard is heard off-screen insisting that the camera cut right there. He soon enters the frame to explain why, *You've got to understand that you're dealing with an image of a 14-year-old child. . . . You're dealing with a little black kid, and let her be a kid. She done answered it with a lot of confidence. Leave that alone!*

The Williams family had to keep insisting on Venus and Serena's girlhood precisely because they understood that Black youth have never been regarded as children in American popular imagination. From the treatment of the Williams girls to the murder of Black boys by law enforcement, Black children are treated as suspect rather than assumed—as white kids are—to be innocent. In fact, Black children have been historically positioned, often in grotesque and violent depictions, against white children as a way to shore up the idea of "childhood innocence" in the service of whiteness and white supremacy.

Venus and Serena were not legible as girls, much less luminous diva girls. Instead, they were derided simply as divas much in the way that Black women have often been labeled as divas—in an effort to diminish rather than applaud their discipline and talent, to mark their racial otherness and sexual excess, and to punish them for being so unapologetically good at what they do. Diva girls, in contrast, were celebrated only if—like Hannah Montana—they sparkled with whiteness and their sparkle was tempered by ordinariness. In this way, diva girls' relationship to celebrity was no different from other forms of stardom that rely on the creation of white glamour through the alchemical tension between specialness and ordinariness.

So, when Venus and Serena sought out ordinary lives as teenaged girls—choosing to attend school and make friends rather than submit to the all-consuming juniors tennis circuit—they were met with doubts and dismay rather than stories of how they were "just like us." And when Serena and Venus each embraced her own specialness, neither sister playing the role of the ordinary sidekick to the other's extraordinary performing girl, when they made room for each other in the spotlight, when they refused to be just like the other tennis girls, they were met with more doubts and dismay. How dare they suggest that Black girls could be diva girls and that more than one of them could command the court? How dare they make folks ponder the possibility that if there's more than one of them, there could be legions of other ordinary Black girls who possess extraordinary performing skills? Diva girl, then, became the latest way to ostensibly celebrate and publicize girls in an effort to shore up white femininity. Diva girl as a blinding flash. As ordinary as a camera bulb.

The year following Indian Wells, from June 2002 to January 2003, Serena will go on to win four consecutive Majors titles—French Open, Wimbledon, US Open, and Australian Open—becoming the first player to win four consecutive major titles since Steffi Graf in 1994, and coining the term *Serena Slam*. In each of the finals for these tournaments, Serena will play Venus. They will grow up and keep winning in the face of racist calls from fans and chair umpires and line judges and reporters. They will win without sacrificing it all—their childhood or diplomas or family ties or fashion lines or psyches or self-regard—much to the chagrin of fellow and former players and all who had long believed individual achievement required such sacrifice. They will win while showing love and support for one another's triumphs, refuting the tokenist notion that either one of them is a singular exception to her people. They will win in their spectacular and often derisively regarded self-designed outfits, as sparkling diva girl denim lines and toys and cosmetics and films and television shows and summer camps and fashion tips are championed all around them. They will win amidst all these blinding flashes.

My girl's wide awake, babbling and whimpering to herself in her crib. It's the last days of the summer of 2009. I'm trying to teach her how to sleep on her own, how to soothe herself when she's feeling fussy. I'm trying to prepare her for this world. This world into which she was born as a brown girl. *The Sisters vs. The World*. I tell her that it's OK to let it all out, the screaming and crying and language-shattering outburst. Sometimes that's what we need after a long, hard day.

I'm learning how to mother a brown girl born into "Generation Diva." So, I do what many other reasonable, concerned Black and brown moms I know do. I watch tennis. I cheer on Serena as she advances through the first few rounds of the US Open that year. But on the day of the semifinals round, I've turned off the television so I can try to doze on the couch while the baby struggles into her nap. I miss it when it happens. The infamous "foot fault" call against Serena and her infamous reaction to it on September 12, 2009. By the end of the year, Serena will be ranked number 1 (again) and will break the record for the highest amount of prize money earned by a female tennis player in one year—thanks largely to her and her sister's efforts to demand equal pay for women, including a 2006 opinion piece Venus wrote for *The Times* (London) on the eve of Wimbledon that year. But for all these undeniably impressive feats, this year will be remembered by many as the year Serena lost her temper on the court.

Serena was once again playing Kim Clijsters. After losing the first set, Serena smashed her racket on the court. She was given a warning for her outburst; a second violation would cost her a point. Clijsters was up 6–5 in the second set and was

Diva Girl Mad Libs® Erasure Poem: You Go, Girl!
Part Two

only two points away from winning the match. It was Serena's serve; she hit it into the net on her first try, and on her second, the lineswoman called a "foot fault," claiming that Serena's foot had touched the baseline before she completed her serve. It's a call that's rarely made in Grand Slam tennis, and never made to decide a match. It cost Serena a point.

This certainly wasn't the first time Serena faced a controversial call. In fact, it was as a result of the five glaringly bad calls made against her by tennis umpire Mariana Alves in 2004 that "Hawk-Eye," a line-calling technology system, was implemented at the US Open. No, it wasn't the first time, nor would it be the last. But it was the first time Serena lost her temper at a major tournament in response to a questionable call during the course of play. *I swear to God I'm fucking going to take this fucking ball and shove it down your fucking throat, you hear that?* The outburst, following the warning Serena had received earlier, gave Clijsters another point, ultimately costing Serena the match. *I swear to God.*

It wasn't her finest moment. But maybe it was the moment of release that made it possible for her to come back another day. Maybe it was a moment of self-preservation that enabled her eventual longevity. I admit that when I finally watched the footage, I shouted out similar obscenities at the officials, not unlike many of the other reasonable, concerned Black and brown moms I knew. We had, after all, watched Serena and Venus grow up and felt a shared sense of maternal protectiveness toward them, even if some of us were only old enough to be their big sisters. We had, after all, watched Serena and Venus withstand—with composure and unapologetic athletic prowess—the racist taunts and doubts and disregard over so many years. It's not that I easily overlook or forgive all of Serena's faults. (I still shake my head with disappointment when I remember watching Serena from the stands at the US Open Women's Finals in 2019, as she played poorly, relinquishing her chance at capturing a record-breaking twenty-fourth Grand Slam win.) But her heated response to that foot fault call seemed to me—at least as a new mom to a brown girl—so, well, reasonable. *As offensive as her outburst is,* poet Claudia Rankine writes about Serena's response, *it is difficult not to applaud her for reacting immediately to being thrown against a sharp white background.*

I mean how much can a girl take over the years? A girl who has absorbed all those boos and bad calls and bad press, a girl who was never regarded as a girl, much less a girl with feelings? What would have happened if Serena had been acknowledged as a girl, celebrated unequivocally for her wondrous diva girl skills, or at least allowed on occasion to express herself as a justifiably angry, ordinary Black girl? What's the woman who was never seen as a girl to do?

What's the mother of a brown girl born into all these blinding flashes to do?

I want to fucking teach my girl how to hit the shit out of a fucking ball so she won't shove it down someone's fucking throat.

Shortly after my daughter's second birthday, I drive to the big-box store and buy a sparkly racket—the only "color" available for a toddler girl player—and snap photos and cheer as Frank gives our girl her first tennis lesson on the public courts in our neighborhood. I swear to God.

First tennis lesson

9

Diva Revivals

Me and Ms. (Jomama) Jones

The first time I saw Jomama Jones, I wasn't ready. I made no record. Not a snapshot. Not a diary entry. Not a smudged note scribbled with eyeliner on the back of a program. The October sky was a gray slate. And then she appeared. I recall a certain radiance—a deep purple sequined minidress that covered only just enough to show off the full length of her Tina Turner-esque legs that rolled us down the river all night. I didn't see it coming.

It was the fall of 2009, deep in the heart of Texas. Jomama Jones was performing a one-night-only concert as part of the Fire and Ink Cotillion, a weekend-long festival for Black queer writers who made up a large share of the audience that Saturday night. I didn't know much about her except what I'd read in the promotional materials: *Jomama Jones is a living legend. Born in Hardtimes Mississippi City, USA, Jones took the top of the charts with hits like "Ghetto (In My Mind)" and "Afromatic." Her solo career led her across oceans and into the hearts of dancers, lovers, and the socially engaged alike.* I knew she had recently come back—

so the story went—from a decades-long exile in Switzerland and that she was on tour promoting her comeback album, *Lone Star*. I knew, from the moment the spotlight shined on her voluminous afro and silver platform boots, that she seemed to have come back as much from the future as from the past. And I knew that she was the alter ego, the "drag" persona, the conjuration—or "cousin," as she would tell it—of the playwright and performer Daniel Alexander Jones. Which didn't diminish her—or his—realness.

I, too, had come back earlier to the Lone Star state after a decade-long self-imposed exile. A handful of years in, and I was still trying to find my way back. That autumn I found myself struggling to come back to my poetry after a prolonged absence during all those singularly focused years I'd spent in the various stages of becoming a scholar: finishing a dissertation and then a book all in the hopes of securing tenure. The October sky was a gray slate. And I was trying to write my way back.

I was trying to come back to the fuller body of my work, to my own altered body after having given birth that spring, after enduring one too many (that is, one) "Mommy and Me" gatherings with middle-class (former) professional women who carried their babies close to their bodies all day (because, of course, the women in Africa do it!), who took pride in all-natural and organic production and consumption, and who spoke with self-congratulatory relief about their decisions to relinquish their careers for motherhood (Inc.) in which they served as CEOs of their children's lives. Apparently, I had become a mother during an economic recession in which experts insisted that so many of our problems could be solved, not (God forbid!) by structural changes, but by each individual middle-class mother's (delusion of) choice to apply her market skills exclusively at home, to disavow all that second-wave feminist nonsense about "having it all," to aspire to be (as the neol-

ogism of the time proclaimed) a mompreneur. I wasn't ready
for this. I wanted to come back.

I recall a certain radiance—Jomama singing, *I'm a lone star
/ flying through the midnight sky / Pin your wish on me.* I looked
into the darkness and followed this lone star: a diva showing
me how to understand and undertake a comeback.

REVIVAL
[*noun*] · re·viv·al · /rə'vīvəl/
1. an instance of something becoming popular, active, or
   important again
   synonym: comeback, resurgence   *rhymes with*: arrival
   as in: The revival of Ms. Jomama Jones teaches us about
   the timelessness and timeliness of the diva.

That night at the Fire and Ink Cotillion, Jomama strutted
back and forth and back again across the mostly unadorned
stage as she sang "Endless Summertime," the first song on her
Lone Star album. Her swaying arms, the bounce in her step,
and the lyrics all embodied the delights and gestures of Black
urban play from the 1970s and 1980s: *Out on the corner jumpin'
double dutch / Skaters got that magic touch . . . / Short shorts and
my afro puffs / Show y'all that I got the stuff.*

But even as she located us in a specific time and place, even
as she pulled loose the thread of our nostalgia, she pulled us
in another direction as well. She strode and bucked and smiled
at us knowingly as she transformed the counting and clapping game rhythms of girls' outdoor play into an anthem of
unbounded sexual pleasure:

One Two Three and Four
Are you gonna open up your door?
Fee Fi Fo Fum
Are you gonna let Jomama get some?

Two Four Six Eight Ten
When we get done we're gonna do it again . . .

Musically, the song begins with a bright escalation of notes on the vibes for a few measures that transports us back to the popular musical sounds of the '70s and '80s—Roy Ayers's "Everybody Loves the Sunshine" comes to mind—while also offering a lightness and propulsion that carries us forward, that insists not just on a memory of lost pleasures but on an endless indulgence in pleasure. The song and Jomama's loose and unloosed gestures—the strut, the sway, the bounce—brought, brings (what tense are we in, really?) all those feelings of free time back to us only to extend time beyond the then and now. Even at the end, the refrain, *Endless Summertime / Dancing in the corners of my mind*, buoyed by the vibes, repeats over and over and over again. It could go on forever.

I didn't want it to end and neither did the students I had taken along with me to Jomama's performance that October night. So, I invited Daniel—or was it Jomama?—to visit our class on divas later that week. I didn't know what would happen or who would show up. But I did know that the possibilities were, well, endless.

Our classroom was just like any other found in a large, public university theatre department. Drab functionality on the edges of disrepair. Hard plastic chairs, a window busted shut, the chalkboard a gray slate. And then she appeared, wearing a bold-print wrap dress that fit her in ways that would have made Diane von Furstenberg weep with joy. Jomama joined us as we pulled our chairs into a circle. She sat on the same chairs that we did, legs crossed at the ankle, black patent peep-toe heels gleaming. But unlike the rest of us, she sat in her chair with an effortlessly erect posture and maintained it throughout our time together. I recall a certain radiance, an ease with which she inhabited her pedagogical role and the

classroom space, never acting above her environs even as she
lifted us beyond it.

That afternoon, Jomama told us a story about a divine,
mythical being who transforms herself and who at (and *on*)
every stage of her development wields tremendous power.
She was talking about Mothra, the benevolent and monstrous
creature, who in her various forms—mammoth egg, voracious
larva, silken cocoon, or vibrant winged imago—fiercely pro-
tects those who worship her. Frequent opponent of Godzilla,
Mothra is humanity's guardian monster. She saves us from
the forces that seek to destroy us. She encourages us to draw
on our strengths no matter what phase of our growth we find
ourselves in. In a constant state of transformation, she is less
concerned with arrival than with revival. Even at the end: the
moment of Mothra's death is invariably followed by a scene of
her offspring hatching. A comeback is always imminent.

The year I met Jomama I was struggling to come back from
what I had believed to be my failures at motherhood. My body

Jomama delivering her diva   *Jomama nurturing an admiring*
lessons   *young fan*

couldn't quite get the hang of it. Breastfeeding never worked out for me. Which might have been fine if this were the '70s of my own childhood when no-nonsense, working(-class) women like my mother just bought formula. I was clearly out of step with my time, with the twenty-first-century insistence on "intensive mothering" and its child-centered, expert-guided, labor-intensive, financially expensive glorification of self-abnegation and consumption as the markers of maternal triumph and as the remedy for the increasing withdrawal of state-sponsored structural support for families. I could not keep time with the rhythms of a historical moment in which working moms were (lauded for) spending more time caring for their kids than mothers did back in 1965 when the majority of them stayed at home. And at my apparently "advanced maternal age," I was running out of time to discipline my body for this task.

I failed. And worse, I came to believe I was a failure. I was done with natural. I longed for something as artificial as infant formula. For the creative application of artifice. For something real.

So, I turned to other feminine and feminist artists who had found a way to make a hard-fought comeback with their voices and their bodies not just intact but inviolable. By which I mean I followed Jomama to New York a year after she visited my divas class. She was premiering a new show, *Radiate*, on December 29, 2010, at Soho Rep, a downtown theatre known for showcasing innovative new work by contemporary artists and for attracting audiences under the age of 40. Never mind that I was already 40. I joined the swarms of followers.

Radiate was framed as a full-length comeback concert directed by Kim Moore and described in the promotional materials as the return of the mythical R&B diva Jomama Jones, *back from the darkness as a lone star with a singular purpose—to awaken the comeback in us all!* During the course of the performance, Jomama relayed the story of her departure and return while showcasing a wide stylistic range of songs—disco, electronic, R&B, new wave, and torch song ballads—co-written with her collaborator, Bobby Halverson, and an equally dazzling array of costume changes—from sequined shift dresses to floor-length feathered ball gowns designed by Oana Botez-Ban and Ron Cesario. Through it all, the Sweet Peaches—Helga Davis and Sonja Perryman—sang and danced along with Jomama across a minimalist, curtain-draped set designed by Arnulfo Maldonado.

Jomama made the space she inhabited seem both smaller and more expansive all at once. She moved across styles and genres and gender categories, pushing beyond the recognizable boundaries of a cabaret act or a tribute concert or an off-Broadway show. She worked both with and against the conventional theatrical setting of a proscenium stage and raked seats by occasionally walking offstage or playfully coaxing an audience member or two (or more) onstage while she recounted the adventures along the way to her comeback or delivered a diva lesson. Throughout her flirtatious banter and the dissolution of theatrical boundaries, she stayed in the spotlight, maintaining an impenetrable composure. Utterly whole. Inviolable.

In *Radiate*, Jomama fleshed out the signature diva persona and genre-blurring performance style that I had first glimpsed in the *Lone Star* concert and that would come to characterize her shows to follow: cabaret's genteel intimacy combined with performance art's total immersion, the sly wink of drag anchored by an earnest and loving devotion to Black female artistry. All shimmering under the reflected lights of the mirrored disco ball that spun above the stage like a moon in orbit around a celestial body of greater gravitational force.

The story of Jomama's comeback is as much factual as it is fictional. Daniel Alexander Jones first performed as Jomama briefly during the mid-1990s, but as he describes it, *by 1997*,

Jomama radiates

I'd packed her up and tucked her away. I didn't know that as I cycled through many versions of myself, so too did this Time Lady who was still becoming, waiting for her return. She came back to him in 2009. *Like how comets go away and then come back*, Daniel recalls, summoned, in part, by the tentative hopes offered by the inauguration of the Obama era. *She's back*, a reviewer for the *Village Voice* noted with delight, traveling *"incog-negro" to take the pulse of Obama's America (and give concerts)*. Jomama returned both in and out of time, timely and timeless.

Daniel establishes Jomama's backstory through a series of fictionalized (or are they?) cover stories featured in Black popular magazines such as *Jet* and *Black Beat* and *Rock & Soul* (known for their exclusive focus on Black artists in an era when more mainstream outlets like *Tiger Beat* and MTV still only featured white artists). There's a collaged cover of *Rock & Soul* that features a photo of Jomama among shots of Michael Jackson, Prince, Diana Ross, and DeBarge. Here is Jomama literally at the center of explicitly Black musical artists and traditions of 1970s and '80s R&B, soul, disco, and house. How can we not feel as if we remember her there and then?

In the three-page-long *Black Beat* interview, "Jomama Jones: Every Second Counts," April Rogers, an admiring and eager (and mythical) reporter, captures a moment with Jomama backstage while on tour in San Francisco in 1983. Within just two columns of the interview, Jomama rapturously extols the artistry of many of her popular diva contemporaries, lauding Stacy Lattisaw's music, Tina Turner's cover of "Let's Stay Together," Nona Hendryx's new album, and anticipating her upcoming attendance at Diana Ross's now famous 1983 Central Park concert. In response to April's earnest questions about a song from her repertoire, "Afraid to Dream," Jomama gracefully instructs that the song was written by Josephine Baker and that she sings it as a tribute to the legendary diva. She then follows up this anecdote with a story of two recent

---

backstage visitors who made her nervous from awe: Sylvester (*so . . . dazzling*) and Martina Navratilova (*her athleticism is just the tops*).

This litany of names conveys the diva lineage from which Jomama, and Daniel, descend, insisting on a stance of diva fandom rather than simply diva enactment that is at the heart of her (and Daniel's) artistry. Here is Jomama in 1980s San Francisco, proclaiming admiration for Nona and Sylvester and Martina—all of whom were never straight but always on target and all of whom were, like Jomama, both before and of their time. Here is Jomama located in a queer time and place marked by diva bodies enacting astonishing musical and bodily feats against the descending shadows of the AIDS crisis. Here is Jomama framed both thematically and literally by affirmations of Blackness, her photo floating above an advertisement for hair dye that promises, *No More Gray, The Easy Way. Be Gone. **Jet Black**.* Jomama Jones: resolutely black, jet black.

The headlines of the (fabricated) October 30, 1983 *Jet* magazine cover story announce Jomama's world tour within the context of a story that asks, "Blacks in Politics: Will 1984 Change the Game?" This question is, of course, a knowing wink to the last Black candidate to run for president before Barack Obama: Jesse Jackson, with his Rainbow Coalition campaign in his first bid for the presidency in 1984. Here is Jomama framed by this historic moment of post–civil rights Black aspiration, evoking a tradition of the Black diva participating as a central figure in the pronouncements of Black striving for political and cultural power. This archive of Jomama doesn't just offer up her individual backstory but also puts the moment of her comeback in 2009 within historical context, reminding us that the Obama victory didn't come out of nowhere or signal a new post-racial break from the past but was in fact a culmination of so many previous Black struggles and aspirations. Here is Jomama's backstory as a cautionary tale for the present: the hopes for more expansive Black cultural and political representation are dashed in the years following 1984, marked by Jackson's defeat and Jomama's (fictional) departure. The cover is as much asking "Blacks in Politics: Will 2009 Change the Game?" as it is interrogating the past. Jomama Jones: timely and refusing to be bound by a linear, teleological ordering of time.

I arrived at Soho Rep on the last day of the year. It was 2010, and I was there for a special New Year's Eve preview performance of *Radiate* before it launched its official January 4–15 run. I remember the journey, first a bus and then a train from the northern reaches of the Bronx to the crowded streets of the Village and then back again in the early hours of the next morning. The moon that night was a waning crescent, the last phase before the unpunctured blackness of the new moon.

The stage was encircled by gauzy curtains in a perfect cylinder like the beam of a spaceship signaling its landing. I found my seat and began reading the souvenir program book I had bought that included song lyrics, dramaturgical notes, a short essay about Jomama's status as a diva, an interview with Daniel, and the recollections of concert producer Christian John Wikane, who fleshed out Jomama's backstory with a description of her nocturnal and musical migrations back in the day:

> *Anyone living in the West Village in summer 1984 certainly remembers how the promotional posters for the "Electrify" single adorned building facades along 7th Avenue South. Her music bridged enclaves that were typically stratified. On any given night, she'd appear uptown at the Lenox Lounge in Harlem, serving up the quiet storm portion of her repertoire, before hopping a limousine downtown to perform at the Paradise Garage, a place that accorded Jomama the same reverence as another Jones (Grace, that is).*

Soon, the Sweet Peaches drew back the curtains and Jomama sauntered in from upstage center wearing a silvery-white loose-fitting low-cut scoop-neck tank dress scooped even lower down her muscled back.

I recall a certain radiance—Jomama in opalescent sequins, lustrous as mother-of-pearl. Mighty Afro-dite, indeed. She's flanked by Davis in her fierce columnular androgyny and Perryman in her curvaceous feminine gravitas, the trio grapevining in sync across the stage as they harmonized on the evolving chorus of the cri de coeur, "Out of Time": *Free free free / You don't want us to be. . . . Free free free / Running out of time. . . . Free free free / That's what we'll be. . . . Free free free / Now you're out of time.* The lyrics and electric guitar–driven propulsive beat of this song blast out and put on blast the forces that curtail Black freedom. The song's frenetic rhythms and insistent repetitions assert an urgency that the time for Black freedom is overdue and issue forth an Afro-future where that freedom may flourish.

Jomama sang and sauntered and I was filled with longing for the shuttered downtown nightclubs and with the sense that I was being transported to a time and place beyond what I had allowed myself to live—the life of a poet in New York, as Lorca once wrote. What I was feeling was not the submission to nostalgia's regressive regime but the uprising of something more mutinous. I was feeling an awakening of previously foreclosed potential. I was feeling the pull of a migration across the city's racial divides (from the Lenox Lounge to the Paradise Garage, from the Bronx to SoHo), across musical genres (from New Wave pulse to piano lounge torch song), across the discrete boundaries of time and space beyond those milky curtains. A sense of revival, of impending arrival. A comeback.

Early on in the show, Jomama revealed that she had fled the country over two decades earlier because her record company did not support the politics and (Black) power she expressed in her records:

> *I had a really intimidating 'fro at that point and everyone*
> *was saying—because that was the time of the jheri curl—*
> *they said to me, "You need to relax your lyrics, relax your*
> *image, you're just too hard and pointed.". . . Then they*
> *asked me to relax my hair. And that's when I ripped up my*
> *contract in front of them.*

The story of Jomama's refusal to compromise her politics and aesthetics for the recording industry and her subsequent exile to the Swiss Alps summons the story of Tina Turner, who (like Josephine Baker and Nina Simone), after her comeback, moved to Europe, where she settled and eventually gained citizenship in Switzerland. Like Tina, Jomama's departure and return honors a tradition of Black divas whose comebacks model a hard-earned ownership over their artistic identity and a sense of time outside a capitalist logic of productivity or linear progression that is often especially damaging for women. They insist on being *out of time.*

The diva is often synonymous with the comeback, which should come as no surprise, since one of her signature features is the ability to endure with flair and with her ever-evolving talents intact. And while the diva is not the only one known for coming back—athletes like Michael Jordan and Magic Johnson come to mind—there is something noteworthy about a female figure defying the tyranny of misogynist time and insisting on her value and virtuosity past her so-called prime.

No stranger to struggle, the diva makes no secret of the countless and often sexist or at least gendered trials she faces on her way to the protective warmth of the stage lights. It is not that she rises above suffering, but that she makes an art of moving through it with style. She does not succumb. She is, as

Ms. Jones sings, *a lone star flying through the midnight sky.* Jomama's songs and her virtuosic perseverance transport us beyond our own despair and isolation. She holds us in the capacious wake of her movements, she holds to her convictions, she holds out hope for a sense of redemption for the rest of us fighting to get back on our feet, to repair and return to the sanctity of our bodies and our voices. We pin our wish on her, knowing she'll carry it high. She is singular, the lone star, and she is as vast as a galaxy.

Divas hold us and they let us loose. On the final night of the year 2010, after the last encore, Jomama invited us to descend from our raked seats at Soho Rep to dance with her onstage. Together we moved through the space between the old year and the new one, and as our bodies shook and shimmied so hard we failed to hear the clock strike twelve, I was reminded of mythical reporter April Rogers's observation about Jomama's performances at the end of her *Black Beat* interview: *You don't know how much time is passing when she is onstage. It's kind of a drag when the show is over.* But in those moments before, time comes and goes and comes back again. Nothing about it drags.

REVIVAL

[*noun*] · re·viv·al · /rə'vīvəl/

2. a restoration to bodily or mental vigor, to life or consciousness

   synonym: recovery, resuscitation   *rhymes with*: survival

   as in: Jomama Jones doesn't drag the dead but instead offers a reverent revival of iconic Black divas of the past.

In response to a question about how gender informs the creation of his work, Daniel once said, *I feel like I'm a little girl who's friends with a little boy, and both are inside of this man who is waiting for this goddess to come back from the moon.* In some ways, his answer reflects the underlying ethos of drag: the gender fuckery, the reliance on a divine feminine figure as the source of inhabitation, the sense of queer time marking the expression of his age(s). But he goes on:

> *Jomama to me is of another dimension and she comes through, and the closest thing that I can say is that she is a kind of very personalized and secularized version of an energy that might be best analogous to an Orisha. She arrives when the ritual space is created. . . . And then when she's done, she goes away. And, so my relationship with her is like an acolyte. I tend the temple, you know? And I wait for her to come back.*

His comparison of Jomama to the Yoruba deity figure of an Orisha roots Jomama and his relationship with her in African traditions of worship and study. He is her follower. He clears the space for her return from the celestial beyond and not simply from the dead. The ritual: less drag than conjuration. *She is my alter-ego*, Daniel has been known to say, *but really, she is my altar-ego*. He is at her service and not the other way around, as is often the case in some conventional practices of drag that summon the aging (rather than ageless) diva to fashion a catty stance of belittlement rather than expansion. He is in thrall to her, looking up to her for inspiration and insight rather than looking down on her as he drags her back to the stage.

I keep coming back to Jomama's legs: sleek and brown and toned and trained as Tina Turner's. Jomama strides downstage at the opening of *Radiate* in a sequined tank shift dress with a low neck and a high hemline that showcases the sheen and sinew of her sculpted arms and impossibly long legs. She struts, she shimmies, she squats, she stands tall. And she does it all sincerely. She comes to life the way Tina Turner came (back) to life in the 1980s: simply the best. Not aging but ageless. Not garish, but groomed. And galloping ahead.

Jomama and her Sweet Peaches galloping ahead

I keep coming back to the verve and reverence that ani-
mate Daniel's embodiment of Jomama. I'm not alone. I'm in
a chorus singing our praise songs. David Rooney, in his *New
York Times* review, writes that *within the alternative-drag spec-
trum of other downtown theater staples, Mr. Jones does not go for
the comic jugular in the manner of Justin Bond's Kiki DuRane.*
Jill Dolan as the *Feminist Spectator* praises Daniel's *lightly worn*
drag in which *he's not "crossing" gender so much as embracing a
femininity that's as much a part of him as masculinity.* In the *New
Yorker*, Hilton Als admires the ways *Jones didn't treat Jomama
as an accessory attached to his drag; he embodied her with the kind
of humility that is often absent from those contemporary performers
who deal with gender in their work.* And then there's my friend,
Clare Croft, a queer performance critic who saw the show

with me one night and who usually finds femininity suspect but who exclaimed after Jomama's show, *I think I understood lipstick for the first time tonight.*

This is not our mother's camp, or *Mother Camp*, as feminist scholar Esther Newton once famously wrote. No parody of the dead (or near-dead) diva brought back as zombie spectacle or whiskey-soaked banshee (think: Judy Garland impersonators). Nor is it the neutered mainstream version of drag evacuated of its disruptively sneering queer critique while holding tight to its racist ideals of glamour and fear of femininity (think: John Travolta in 2007 rather than Divine in 1988, in *Hairspray*). Not a dead or deadening force. A live wire.

In conjunction with the opening of *Radiate* in December 2010, Soho Rep posted a video called "Jomama Jones Explains Her Diva Influences." What I find most striking about the video is that it is from Jomama's perspective, not Daniel's. It is both "in drag" and out beyond its limits. Instead of replaying the tired scene of a gay man putting a diva to catty or cutting use (one that persists even among some of the queens competing on *RuPaul's Drag Race*, which premiered the same year as Jomama's *Lone Star* concert), the video stages a diva figure loving other divas without irony or parodic competitiveness. *Jones didn't use Jomama as a metaphor to talk about his anger or hatred or misogyny*, Hilton Als writes, *It was clear he loved her, and it made us love him.* It was clear Jomama loved other divas, and she made us love them, too.

In the video Jomama's voice narrates over archival clips of performances by Josephine Baker, Lena Horne, Billie Holiday, Angela Bofill, Tina Turner, and the women of Labelle: Patti LaBelle, Nona Hendryx, and Sarah Dash. Jomama speaks reverently about their performance styles, vocal power, personal triumphs, and political activism. Her devotional tone and attentiveness make the video not simply promotional but pedagogical: Jomama charts her diva ancestry—referring to Baker and Horne as *my own fairy godmothers*—and also models for us how to read and revere the rigorous training and ineffable charisma emanating from divas. She admires Horne's *extraordinary dignity*; she urges us to observe how Holiday is *listening with her skin* and how Turner has *honed herself into top form like a boxer*. She intones that Labelle *meets us with a gaze that comes from the depths of their spines*.

Jomama's relationship to divadom and Daniel's departure from conventional drag is clearly expressed in Jomama's admiration for Angela Bofill, the Harlem-born Afro-Cuban and Puerto Rican R&B and jazz singer popular during the 1970s and 1980s. Bofill's video image shimmers in a baby blue dress, her eyes heavy-lidded and shadow-frosted, her voluminous hair fastened on one side with a signature flower. Jomama sees her *as a contemporary, but one who was a teacher. She just had a way of combining the history of all of those wonderful artists we've looked at so far with something extraordinarily of the moment and contemporary. She was fresh like the flower you see in her hair.*

Jomama lauds the talents of someone she considers a living peer and not a dead predecessor, modeling for us how a pedagogical relationship rather than a competitive one might be imagined among contemporaries. Jomama teaches us how to elevate a lesser acknowledged artist into the pantheon of established divadom. She revels in the repetition with revision—simultaneously *combining the history* and being *of the moment*—that characterizes Bofill's artistry. Of course, she is talking at once about Bofill and about herself. Jomama revisits and revives and revises the sensibilities and gravitas and *freshness* of iconic Black divas rather than making fetishized spectacles of their struggles or suffering or mortality. *Fresh like the flower you see in her hair.*

Jomama and her Sweet Peaches are the grown-up "Space Children" that Labelle once sang about on their legendary

1974 album, *Nightbirds.* Jomama steely and sleek as the Chrysler Building, Helga all asymmetrical androgynous angles, and Sonja all sweetness and curves like meringue atop a tart pie. Jomama's lyrics propel us forward, and her music pulls us pleasurably back to Labelle's R&B, soul, funk, house, and disco sounds of the 1970s. *Radiate* is what Afro-futurism sounds like now: pulsing toward *what was and what if,* moving between *terrestrial insurrection* and *extraterrestrial hope.* Jomama and her Sweet Peaches evoke Labelle's sonic sensibility that showcases Black female voices converging in exquisite harmonies in one moment and diverging in the next as they share the lead or pull in multiple directions from the melody. Radiating the harmonies of a closed fist, of an open heart, of all that we seek together to lift up.

The tender admiration that suffuses Daniel's conjuration of Jomama and all the divas from whom she descends reminds me of the earnest devotion and musical virtuosity of John Kelly's inhabitation of Joni Mitchell or the studied contraction and release of Richard Move's gestures as Martha Graham or the self-fashioning flair of all those brown girls out there who "become" Selena. All of them conjuring something or someone both within and beyond themselves. And, yet, unlike these others, Jomama is not a singular, "historical" diva to whom her acolytes attempt verisimilitude as a means of showcasing their truest selves or their own original talents. In this way, Jomama is not unlike her contemporary, RuPaul, who also creates a Black diva alter ego who acts as a mentor to others and who affirms Black feminine glamour and virtuosity.

In their pedagogical sensibilities, both Jomama and RuPaul descend in many ways from the tradition of Harlem ball drag mothers of the 1980s and 1990s like Pepper LaBeija or Angie Xtravaganza who ruled over their respective, eponymous "houses" in which they sheltered and mentored generations of their drag children (and inspired the FX series *Pose,* which showcased the talents of Michaela Jaé Rodriguez, Indya Moore, Dominique Jackson, and Billy Porter). To be a drag mother in this scene was to be resolutely Black or (and) brown and to refuse to relinquish your crown to your children but instead to model for them your creative expertise, your feminine artistry, your ability to achieve "Realness" through the exquisite application of artifice. Now, here, at last, was a model of motherhood I could get behind.

Jomama and RuPaul, are also, of course, heirs to disco diva Sylvester's gender-bending fabulousness and the ways he made us feel "Mighty Real," the ways he embodied the realness of the best of aspiring Black queens who knew that to feel real was *to make the costume into your own skin, to bring the fantasy self into actual being*. But, whereas RuPaul (like Sylvester) is both the masculine creator and the feminine persona performed, Jomama is less reducible to a singular role as Daniel's other half. She is, as Daniel describes, *a mix of popular icons. Donna Summer, Diana Ross, Tina Turner, and one part historical heir to Josephine Baker. . . . She occupies myth and reality as an original.* Daniel's conjuring of her is an act of collective autobiography of popular Black American divas in all of their radiance. Less drag, more lift. More lift every voice and sing.

Jomama is of a certain age, in every sense of that phrase. She unabashedly affirmed her generational vintage as she made her comeback in the Obama era, and she also evokes a certain past era rooted in the radical Black politics of the 1960s and '70s and in the sonic influences of Black popular music of the 1970s and '80s. She moves across age(s). She goes from Tina Turner–inspired gyrations in a minidress to the disciplined reserve of Lena Horne in a pillar gown.

Near the end of the *Radiate* performance, Jomama appeared in a steely mauve gown with a fitted high-necked halter and A-line skirt that stretched to the floor. It was positively imperial. She assumed the stature of a redwood: rooted in the earth and reaching for the heavens. Ancient and ageless. She assumed the stature of Lena Horne and her disciplined composure honed for decades in those smoky, Jim Crow cabarets. Impervious. Preserved. Like both the redwood and Lena Horne, Jomama assumed the stature of those who surrounded and supported her. In an interview with Eisa Davis printed in the program notes for *Radiate*, Daniel talks about the source of Jomama's stature:

> *I just remember a <u>posture</u>. There's just a posture that was common among black people in my experience—old, young, man, woman, poor, middle class, boojy, whatever—there's a posture that I don't see now. As lively. And so for me, that posture, that spine, that literal spine is the thing that she is.*

Jomama Jones has a spine. Hers is a stance, not of decay, but of preservation. *As lively.* She stands for something more than herself. She is the many in the one. She revives the stance of Black folks of a certain age. She revives, as Abbey Lincoln once sang, *the people in me*, all of them, coming back, coming together. Like a little girl who likes a little boy, and who are both inside a man who is waiting for a goddess to come back from the moon.

REVIVAL

[*noun*] · re·viv·al · /rəˈvīvəl/

3. a reawakening or arousing of religious or spiritual fervor, especially by means of a series of lively evangelistic services

synonym: Amen   *rhymes with*: Alleluia

as in: A fan once described a Jomama Jones concert as *a graceful fusion of organic performance art and glam stylized revival meeting.*

The closing number of *Radiate* was its title song—Jomama and the Sweet Peaches assuring us *our world will radiate* in the face of the future's unknown. But the audience was never ready to go. There was always an encore and the encore was always "Soul Uprising," a song meant to save your soul and move your body, a song driven by the upbeat percussive tempo and redemptive lyrics of a gospel choir praise song: *Whatchu gonna do / When the sky starts falling? / . . . You got to get up / And claim your power / . . . Got to rise up 'cause it's a soul uprising!* And always we rose. Reading the lyrics now, with the command to *stand up*, I can understand how the song might seem like a gesture of cheap theatrical manipulation. But in performance, I am here to testify, there was nothing coercive about it. The song filled the space, harnessing and, well, radiating the energy that had accumulated over the course of our time together. Like Labelle or Sylvester, Jomama took us to church and to the dance floor and to the great beyond all at once. She moved us across time and space. She moved us to raise up our hands in praise and to climb over our seats at Soho Rep to dance together onstage. It was, after all, *part concert, part revival*, just as the promotional ads had promised. *In a stellar instant*, Daniel will later write about this moment, *a community became visible. Ephemeral and tender, it would dissipate when the doors opened, but as we danced, oh, how brightly it burned.*

In the ensuing years since my first encounter with Jomama, I was still struggling to come back to my own voice. And I was struggling to raise a daughter who could learn to assert her own. I had leapt off of the conventional timeline marking mid-career success and mid-life security. I had given up tenure. I had given up home ownership. I had long given up on breastfeeding. I had given up on anything resembling intensive mothering or leaning in. I had left Texas and moved back to New York in 2015. I had accepted a teaching position that encouraged me to forge a renewed relationship with my writing. I had ignored well-meaning mommy blogs and had let my six-year-old girl watch *Burlesque* instead of *Beauty and the Beast* (again!) because, well, it passed the Bechdel test and because, well, if a girl's going to learn something about how to make her voice endure, why not learn it from a diva?

I was a believer in search of diva guidance. So, I suppose it's no surprise that I turned and returned to Jomama, the divine figure praised by one reviewer as *a spiritual mother for the moment*. Like any fervent believer searching for some measure of transcendence, I followed her. Jomama followed up *Radiate*'s sold-out run at Soho Rep with a national tour. And in October 2015, she premiered *Black Light*, a show featuring origi-

Jomama in Black Light

nal songs and promoted as *a revival for turbulent times*. I kept coming back, responding most of all and like so many others to the revivalist sensibility of Jomama's call. To the ways her performance and musical styles draw from the Black spiritual tradition of the tent revival to summon and sustain a sense of shared redemption among her fans.

Once when I asked Jomama about what revival meant to her, she moved from the secular to the sacred and back again, remembering how *Ma Rainey would pitch a tent and they would have a blues tent and people would come from all over.* Jomama made explicit her link to the tradition where blues divas *called for others to respond, and what they were calling you to was to the river, calling you to be baptized, calling you to tell your testimony, calling you to let down your burden, calling you to see one another with new eyes.* And so, as followers of Jomama, we turn to the stranger beside us and meet their gaze and move our bodies closer to one another under the pulsing lights. We rise up, responding to Jomama's call to scale the barricades between cabaret's intimacy and disco's ecstatic insistence on collective deliverance through the beat, between the sacred revivals of the holy crusaders and the secular revivals of Ma Rainey and all the blues queens whose songs call us out of our pain and into our desires.

In the early spring of 2016, nearly seven years after Jomama's visit to my class in Austin, I found myself in another classroom at another institution teaching another course on divas to students in New York City who had entered adolescence under the Obama administration and who understood, though the crocuses were unfolding in the darkness below, that so much and so many were dying: a political era, illusions of progress, our Black brothers and sisters. Winter wore out the spring with its snow-muck. And then she appeared. This time shaking a tambourine.

Jomama arrived in her stylish and voluminous wig and her expertly applied makeup and her strappy gold stilettos, striking her tambourine as she spoke. Which is to say, she arrived with the tools we use to punctuate and amplify our worship of the divine, of the divinely feminine, of the divine feminine figure whose revival, whose comeback, we have come to believe in. How could we not follow her? *One of the things that I felt was really important,* Jomama told us that afternoon, *was to make sure that the work that I did when I came back afforded people an opportunity . . . to be in the room with one another in such a way that the spirit could move.*

The winter after Jomama's visit to my class, in the same month as the inauguration of a newly nefarious political era, I will find myself in the audience at Joe's Pub for a performance of Jomama's *Black Light* (*Be a witness. Join the revival,* the poster urged). The house lights will dim and before long, Jomama will sing, *Can I get a witness / for the need in me?*, her voice encircled by her backup singers and propelled by a bluesy bass line and drums. *Can I get a witness?* Jomama will ask and ask. And I will find myself foraging among the lipstick and vials of perfumed oils and packet of wet wipes and loose crayons and battered compact mirror in the folds of my purse in search of my notepad and pen. *Can I?* The final lyric of the song abbreviated as it meets the rising drums. *Can I?* I'll find what I'm searching for and I'll begin, writing feverishly in the dark.

10

Diva Portals

Nona and Patti and Sarah
and All the Space Children

Are you lonely? Patti calling out and Nona and Sarah echoing a response—*Lonely*—as the horns blare. *Are you
lonely? Lonely.* They ask again. And again.

Are you loneleeeeaaaayyyy, Patti excavating unknown vowels
buried in our isolation.

Can you hear the way her voice spirals up and then lin-
gers in midair with the horns? Can you hear it now entwining
with Nona's and Sarah's voices in their otherworldly melding
to complete the question, *living in a city without a heart?* Did
you miss it? That's OK because here's the chorus again. Come
closer. Listen with me. Are you lonely?

I've stopped counting how many weeks we are into lockdown in New York City. The only time I'm keeping now is the
4/4 time signature of "Are You Lonely?" pounding B minor on
repeat to fill the empty air in the city ravaged by plague. After
the official shelter-in-place announcement on March 22, 2020,
many who had the means fled. The rest of us stayed behind
as the death counts rose and the hospitals ran out of beds for

those struggling to live. We remain, as our people have long done in the forsaken city, waking each morning into our grief and longings, going to work or losing our jobs, making love and art, breaking up or down, calling our mothers, waiting for a lover to call, wiping down the counter with bleach, blowing out the speakers with the sounds of three divas joining their voices in exquisite harmonies.

Patti Labelle, Nona Hendryx, and Sarah Dash, the diva-trinity who make up the genre-defying musical trio Labelle, released the song "Are You Lonely?" on their 1974 album, *Nightbirds*. In her book *Why Labelle Matters*, musician Adele Bertei describes the album as *a body-soakin' fusion of New Orleans funk and soul, space glam, and rock'n'roll. The LP brings us the stomp of the gospel past morphing into a music of liberation and flight—an erotic star-sea of possibilities, where the labor pains of musical Afrofuturism howl out a new sensibility of woman.* A work so large it contains multitudes. The lonely soul and the collective groove. The empty street and the crowded dance floor. The pleas and the answered prayers. *Nightbirds* creatively fused Labelle's myriad musical influences and also blasted them free from anything anyone had ever seen or heard before.

The group had gained initial success as "Patti LaBelle and the Bluebelles" in the early 1960s as a foursome: Sarah, Nona, Patti, and its fourth founding member, Cindy Birdsong. Their look and sound followed the tidy harmonies, strict hierarchies, and stylings of coiffed respectability that characterized popular girl groups of the era like the Supremes. Their early hits, "I Sold My Heart to the Junkman," "Down the Aisle (The Wedding Song)," and "Over the Rainbow," secured their status as the "Sweethearts of the Apollo" and their popularity as a touring act in the Chitlin' Circuit. When Birdsong abruptly left the group in 1967 to join the Supremes, they continued as a trio until Atlantic Records let them go from their contract in 1970. Frustrated with the male-dominated control of the

industry, they asked British record producer Vicki Wickham
to sign on as their manager. Wickham agreed and, together
with Puerto Rican costume designer Larry Legaspi and jewelry designer Richard Ecker, helped "Patti LaBelle and the
Bluebelles" transform themselves into the gloriously space
age, soul-grooving, silver-spangled group, Labelle. Freed from
stiff bouffants and pencil skirts, Labelle made four albums
(including the classic "Gonna Take a Miracle," singing virtuosic harmonies with Laura Nyro) between 1971 and 1973.
But it was *Nightbirds*, released by Epic Records in September
1974, that lifted them and their listeners to new heights. The
album is a majestic triumph: the Temple of the Sun God and
Mount Everest and the moon landing all in one grooved disc.
While the LP is often remembered for its lead single, "Lady
Marmalade," written by Bob Crewe and Kenny Nolan and
sung from a sex worker's point of view, what makes *Nightbirds*
soar are the songs that showcase Nona Hendryx's formidable
and feminist songwriting prowess. Labelle went on to release
two more albums before disbanding in 1976. But many of their
songs like "What Can I Do For You?" and "Gypsy Moths" and
"Are You Lonely" played on in regular rotation at discos and
house parties where Black and brown bodies came together
and danced all night.

Labelle broke open a new way for Black girls to share the
stage and a song. *We really treated it like a band, not a girl group,*
Nona said once in an interview with music journalist Ann Powers, *Three minds, but one mind at the same time. And that did allow
for different things to be said.* The trio refused that triangular
geometry of the Black diva lead backed by her supporting-role
sisters, insisting instead on a sound and shape that leveled
and ultimately blasted off from the ground on which Black
women were positioned to sing. It's not just that they share
the lead or that their voices merge in expansive harmonies—
Nona's nerve-struck bass, Sarah's star-grazing soprano, and

Patti's bellows expanding in every direction of the wind—but that their voices merge in a transformational consummation, in a sacred and profane call-and-response ethos of together-ness that lifts and lifts and lifts us as it climbs until the sound barrier and all other barriers are somehow broken through. A model of diva collectivity.

There are few groups that are as important as Labelle, Jomama Jones insists. *There's no vocalist like Patti LaBelle. There's no figure with the kind of warrior energy like Nona Hendryx had. And the sublime beauty of Sarah Dash. The three of them together, theirs is a sound that's never happened since.* Their vocal blend is the sound of communal ascendance, of Black feminist power, of body and soul and the transcendence of all that we can know or name. Their surprising rhythmic arrangements, their unprecedented mixture of gospel and glam and of sweat and spirit broke the sound barriers dividing musical genres and girl group con-ventions and even time itself. As Bertei writes, *Labelle sang the opening aria of Afrofuturism.* Labelle's outfits reach as far as the sounds they make: headdresses of linked cowry shells cascad-ing over silver space-age body suits, metallic bras topped by feathered capes, androgynous over-sized epaulets and gleam-ing streaks of eye shadow. Nothing about them is ever fixed sonically or visually or temporally and in this way they move us through and beyond Afro-feminist space and time. Black divas as transportation, as a transport station.

The month after the *Nightbirds* release, Labelle performed their now legendary "Something Silver" concert at the Met-ropolitan Opera House on October 6, 1974. Though they weren't the first Black divas to sing at the Met (having been preceded by opera divas Marian Anderson, Mattiwilda Dobbs, Leontyne Price, and Shirley Verrett), they were the first Black musical group to perform on its grand stage. Labelle's ascen-dance occurred in a time of fiscal crisis in New York City. In fact, it was the Met's own financial crisis (they couldn't sustain

Labelle in silver

52-week contracts for their performers, had to cancel new sets and costumes, and drastically cut the upcoming season) that prompted them to turn to popular acts to generate income. By the following October, in response to President Gerald Ford's initial refusal to offer the city federal bailout funds, the *New York Daily News* ran its now infamous headline, *Ford to City: Drop Dead*. The city was broke and broken, and still the people answered Labelle's call and came out like luminescent stars puncturing the darkness. *Within moments of constraint, often linked to the material world of sexism, poverty, and loneliness*, Francesca Royster writes about Labelle, *we find a consistent sonics of flight and transcendence*. They show us the possibilities that can arise when we join our voices in the forsaken city.

Are you lonely? Labelle sings the word "lonely" at least sixty times, though it's hard to say for sure because the song fades out on Patti making a mantra of the word so for all I know she's still singing it. The word repeats with such propulsion and such presence it reaches the point of estrangement: the incantatory force of their voices estranging the word from its meaning, estranging us from our own loneliness. They crack lonely open and crawl inside it to keep us company in our despair. Bertei describes the song as full of *that sonic rage of love utterly unique to their vocal blend*. Their comingled voices are the very sound of communion, the sound transforming the lonely "you" into the "we." The "you" addressed in Labelle's songs is so often not just the singular object of desire but a call to those of us who seek salvation in their music. With Labelle, the "you" is the "we." Can you hear it? How many times do you count them singing the word? Can you hear how their voices divide and multiply and expand the whole? Come closer. Let's listen together. They are meeting us in our isolation, insisting that we look outwards from our lonely lives to bear witness to the loneliness of others and, above all, to do more than bear witness, to touch the lonely strangers among us.

Shall we go outside and join the others? Let's join the chorus of those shouting their sonic rage of love in the streets,
grieving the dead, fighting for the living, no longer afraid to
scream out because we are living in a moment when it seems
the only time a stranger touches another is to kneel on the
neck of a Black man crying out for his mother as he dies in the
street. Stay with me now. Can you hear the call and response
Patti does with the horns starting at minute 1:45 as she repeats
lonely and responds to the blare eleven ululating times? How
her voice touches the saxophone's bleat the way a DJ places her
hand on the vinyl to make us dwell in the scratch?

Stay with me now.

Labelle is clearing the space for us to remain present in the
disaster and is transporting us to outer spaces where we might,
just for a moment, transcend the devastation. Can you hear it?
The song is a portal for the lonely to enter. *Are you lonely?* Can
you hear how they stay with the question? How they insist we
live in the questioning? How the question is the portal's latch?

Open it.

Can you feel something opening? How our arms can open
wide enough to hold it all, the unwed mother, the hungry children, the man at the bodega, the woman on the corner, the
living and the dead. Hold onto me. The ground is shifting.
Let's enter the portal their music makes. Don't you want to
travel to a time and place where we might move with joy and
wild abandon on the ruined streets? Don't you want to know
how our people once made it through the forsaken city? How
they excavated something silver from the blasted mine of the
dark city? Hold my hand. The tethers binding us to the here
and now are breaking. Time to lift off. *Nightbird fly by the light
of the moon, makes no difference if it's only a dream.*

Are you still with me?

We're moving backwards and forward all at once. Like the
DJ's hands on the record. Labelle is pulling us to the past so

we can endure the present and dare to imagine our future. Are you holding on? *Take a look around . . . Space children, are there any others?* Let's walk together on the glittering, trash-strewn streets in the fall of 1974. Let's go to the Met to hear the song again. Let's travel to a place where strangers aren't afraid to touch one another.

Are you lonely? Can you feel me here beside you as we make our landing? Let's not stay strangers for long. It's the blue hour just before dawn. We've still got time to find a place to dance. Let's climb inside the vessel of Labelle's music, the escape pod that delivers us to the outer spaces of our unfettered dreaming or the inner spaces of our sweat-soaked desires or laser-focused scheming. Let's move to their voices sharing the lead, listening to the way they lift each voice higher or deeper in every moment of transfer, the way Patti then Sarah then Nona then NonaPattiSarah then PattiSarahNona then NoSaPaNaaaahhhh steer the ship in a song like "I Believe That I've Finally Made It Home" so that wherever home is—far out or far back or right here right now—we trust they'll take us there. Let's go.

Labelle is like three cherries in a row on the slot machine. Jackpot. Listening to them feels like when you're down to your last pile of cash but you decide to play one more hand and you're dealt a royal flush. That feeling of your desperation giving way to anticipation, of watching the trailing wake of your lifelong pain even as you're pulled forward or in some direction you can't yet name, feeling for once that maybe your luck will keep running and not just run out. You know what I mean? Listening and singing and shimmying to Labelle is as close as dark girls sometimes get to feeling free. Their music is a portal through which we can find our way together across the limits of space and time. Let's find the sweet spot of the beat and ride and ride. Let's make our lonely hearts beat faster. Let's shake the trees until the fruit falls. Let's bite the apple. Let's be the apple for each other.

Labelle broke free from that Motown girl-group mold—the hair sprayed high and stiff, the matching empire waist dresses and satin-gloved hands, the imperial order of lead singer and backup voices harmonizing baby love and maybe maybe maybe and chapel of love and wait a minute and love child and nowhere to run. Not that there's anything wrong with the sparkle of a well-placed tiara or the snap of two perfectly manicured fingers or the swish and rustle of a dress atop a diva's proud stride. Like the ladies we'll meet who stroll along 42nd Street or the ones preening at Sheridan Square, the *Village broads with their narrow hips*, as Audre Lorde described them in a poem from her book *Cables to Rage*. You can always trust a girl who can turn a trick into a treat. Who knows better than these girls the need to be in your body and free from it, too? The ones who know how touch can be a trap or a torch or the space where the words we know can't ever reach, how sometimes touch is just *getcha getcha ya ya da da*.

This is how we touch each other in the forsaken city.

Let's mark the time by the shifting shapes of the moon or the succession of Thursdays when the weekly issue of *The Village Voice* hits the stands. Let's buy this week's copy—September 26, 1974—at the stand on this corner. Do you see the full-page ad sandwiched between pages advertising the Disc-O-Mat record store's wholesale deals and Gil Evans playing piano at the Village Vanguard? *LABELLE AT THE MET. Patti LaBelle, Sarah Dash, and Nona Hendryx ARE Labelle— three nightbirds coming to you with the sweet-tongued sound of silver soul.* The announcement framing three shimmering and shadowy figures sharing a mic and opening their mouths wide: *Labelle in concert: The Metropolitan Opera House, Sunday October 6, 8PM . . . WEAR SOMETHING SILVER.*

Let's empty every pocket and toss aside the sofa cushions and flip the mattress and reach into all the secret stashes until we've gathered up enough to make our way to the box office and hand over $4.50 for the cheap seats. No matter that we'll be up near the rafters because isn't high up where Labelle aims to take us, anyway? *Don't bring me down, Lift me up higher higher higher.*

Let's strut and flutter along the darkening streets, filled with wonder about what's ahead and about how and where to find something silver. Let's wonder together over the meaning of silver soul and what it might mean to feel and hear and sing and live it. Silver, to me, is precious without being pretentious, the stuff of coin and cuff, tintype and tinsel. The instrument designed to break into the body—the scalpel and the bullet—and the sealed machine hurtling past the earth's clogged atmosphere. In the land where my father's from, silver's lodged deep in the earth's blasted crust and silver is the soot and sweat of the smelt. Here in the ruined city, silver's the skyscraper's upper floors and the mica-flecked sidewalks sparkling under flashing neon and a working girl's worn soles. Silver is the spinning disco ball and the ball of mercury rising when the fever's set in. The shuddering jingle jangle on the tambourine of a sister who's caught the spirit and the spur's spiked rowel and the horse bearing the weight of a white man. Silver is the chain link belt bought for a quarter at the secondhand store and swaying as we shimmy on the dance floor. Silver soul is war paint and camouflage and late-night risk and early-hour delight and the frosted fox fur trim on a used coat reimagined into strips of lightning-powered armor. Silver soul is scraping by without sacrificing style.

What's the sheen of the silver in your soul? Are you steel beam and blade's edge, all rope and cling and clang and swishing whip? Or are you wind chime and pinball, glitter and streak? As for me, silver summons the Mexican mines carved into the desert and all of my people who labored there and all that came after and before. For Patti and Nona and Sarah's people, silver is that steady flash of charted stars that led so many to freedom.

Silver tarnishes if left too long without touch.

It's in the steady rhythm of all that rubbing and buffing and polishing, the choreography of hands flexing and shaking until the precious thing they hold is loved to a bright shine, in that alchemical interaction between animal and mineral, that's the moment, to me, when silver meets soul.

The moon will wax to full and begin its journey toward dark renewal by the time we arrive again on the plaza of Lincoln Center with all the other space children. The moon is a waning gibbous, and I've transformed into an Aztec winged serpent with the Pyramid of the Moon as my crown. My wings are framed by wire hangers and covered in crinkled foil and shaken glitter and feathers feathers feathers. My pyramid-crown shaped by carved-away scraps of foam and discarded produce boxes reeking of alleyway smoke breaks and ripe bananas from distant shores.

We hear the silver whistles blowing in the darkness before we see the stand outside the entrance where someone is selling them for a dollar each. How can we resist joining this trilling chorus? Silver soul is the sound made when breath meets metal. Shrilling and cooing and preening and flitting, we spread our wings like nightbirds or gypsy moths, all of us moving together through the veil separating this world and what's on the other side. Not quite like Oz in Technicolor. More like some distant star where raised fists and mambo-hips flash in technosilver.

There's the bearded lady in a waist-cinched silver dress and the brother dressed as a silver-caped Blacula. Here's the silver-studded dykes and the self-proclaimed fags in silver jockstraps and not much else. Here's the long-haired hippie girls with Christmas tinsel twisted into their braids and the high-class dame draped in sequins and floor-length fur.

Tall queens with silver shadow spread all the way up to their arched eyebrows and pretty boys with fluttery silver eyelashes that could lure you in like a spider's shimmering web. Silver knights with breastplates and space girls in silver jumpsuits. Someone with their shapely silver-dipped ass on show and someone else shaking silver-dipped maracas. There's Margo Jefferson and Ellis Haizlip and Nikki Giovanni. There's the ones who are easy to recognize like Bette Midler and Jackie O and Debbie Allen and Cher and those we'll never know who won't live past the plague-ravaged '80s. The ones descending the lobby's red-carpeted marble staircase who are ready for their close-up and the ones scaling each step in the hopes of being taken far out. All the sky-high silver afros and skull-hugging silver helmets. The silver-praise clang of tambourines and the silvery-slick sound of East Harlem Spanish. So many Black and brown folks on our way toward our own dark renewals. Each of us radiating with silver soul like a chalice or a rocket ship or any shiny thing designed to rise or be risen—to the mouth or to the moon or to any luminous body in need of nourishment or exploration.

The program lists the title of Labelle's first set, "Prelude in Silver," and isn't that what we are, what they've summoned us to become? We've all come together inside under the sparkle of the starburst chandeliers. I remember once reading the story about these constellations of dazzling moons and radiating stars, their crystal orbs riding on metal rays reaching out at all angles. They were referred to as sputniks—after that first Soviet satellite—when they were installed in the spring of 1966 guided by a vision to have the new Metropolitan Opera House reflect the space age. And here we are bringing that mission to true fruition.

The lights flicker and ascend and Butterfly McQueen walks onstage and introduces the ladies of Labelle in French and the queens in the house are all aflutter. McQueen is the venerable

actress who bore the burden of the role of Prissy, Miss Scar-
let's maid who knew nothin' 'bout birthin' no babies and who
went on to become a camp favorite. But she's also known by
many in this crowd as a student at City College studying political science or as the Queen of the Field Mice in the production of *The Wiz* that just premiered in Baltimore. A queen of
all of us small, scurrying, and flitting creatures. A queen guiding us toward what's beyond the dust and thicket and crumbs
of our everyday.

Ms. McQueen calls out their names and the space is saturated with the roar and rev of engines blasting from the base
of a rocket. Nona struts in her silver platform boots and Sarah
floats in her wavering silver gown and Patti throws back her
head shaking her silver-streaked hair and they are the mother-
ship and we are the flame trailing below and we are the silver
screws lining the ship's panel—so small but significant in our
roles—and we are shaking loose from our threaded grooves in
the shudder of the blastoff.

Spaaace children, Patti launches us in counterpoint to the
driving bass rhythm and Nona and Sarah jump aboard in harmony until they ride out any doubts or until they show us how
to dwell in it with them, their chorused voices riding along
with the synthesizer and their warnings not to fly too high
alone punctuated by the trumpet's blare to give us time to *take
a look around* at our space sisters and brothers, to take the voy-
age with and through one another. We are the voyagers and
their song tethers us to our common base and we float and spin
within the spacious anti-gravity of their harmonies and some
of us get so free we break what binds us and we tumble and
twirl farther out into the black expanse.

The first act is all this silver ascent but it is also sweat and
funk and growl and moan and a sensorium of earthly pleasure
and toil, of lungs and larynx and nostril and belly and all the
cavities that make and hold and lift the breath, of choir prac-

tice and call-and-response and hymnal descant and all the disciplines of deep listening and embodied union that make and hold and lift the harmonies among three earth-shattering and earth-smoldering voices. Labelle carrying at once the street divas' command of the body—how to wield it and shield it, how to make it work for you and how to work your way out of its binds—and the cosmic diva's shapeshifting force freed at last from the lashed flesh. For even as Labelle is the spaceship and the labor and thrill of its launch, Labelle is also the landing pad for those of us who want to touch down, who seek a redemptive return.

Hello, upstairs, they begin the song that downshifts us from reverie to contemplation, the opening lyrics of "I Believe That I've Finally Made It Home." And in response to their summoning, the young Black children of the Mount Vernon Gospel Chorus file in from the wings to join them onstage, singing and swaying and clapping and suddenly the space is transformed from the silver soul of outer space to the silver soul of belt buckle and holy entreaty and tightly woven plaits and the preteen possibility of a Black future. Labelle's divadom is a kingdom so vast that it can hold us all: the space queen and the stoop kid, the church and the club, the rhythms of synthesizer and double Dutch, the unfettered woman who shapes her mouth until lightning bolts out and the angel-voiced boy seeking shelter from the storm.

Together they sing, assuring us of the sterling truths we know and affirming our desire to be of this world but not entirely in it. The choir singing and singing and singing the lyric, *And I'm all right,* until we all believe we are or at least will be, until we believe we can make it home, can make a home here and now and ever after. This is how we make our home in the ailing city.

Are you still with me? Do you want to touch down? Slip back for a spell to the future, to our ravaged present? Let's go home. Let's play the song again. It's from their 1972 album *Moonshadow* and penned by Nona. Let's turn up the volume and open the windows so it all spills out. Can you hear how they share the lead? Let's follow the sound of their voices, the example they offer. Let's take turns. Now I'll hold it down so you can rest. Now you hold it together so I can weep. Now me. Now you. Now the neighbor who can hear us through the dusty screens holding steady to the sound of Labelle. Can you hear how their voices come together and harmonize on the final chorus? Hear how they are all right while the political world has gone mad? Hear the sound of how we make it through the devastation that surrounds us? Can you feel the vibrations of their voices thrumming through our battered bodies? Can you feel their healing force in this city of plague? Are you listening? Can you hear the clapping? The yelling and pot-banging? It's 7 p.m. in the locked-down city and we are leaning out the opened windows cheering on the ones laboring to save lives at hospitals across the city. Can you see the nurses and bodega cashiers and delivery bikes and ambulances passing by on the streets below? *Passing stranger! you do not know how longingly I look upon you*, Walt Whitman writes, *You must be he I was seeking, or she I was seeking.* Can you hear in Labelle's voices the longing and the seeking and the touching, the grief and the momentary relief?

Let's pass back through. We've only experienced the concert's first act. Let's follow Labelle's voices across Afro-futurist time. Let's return to the Met and polish our silver souls until they shine.

The houselights brighten for intermission, and we are a throbbing hive abuzz with shared vibration, feeling as if our chorused voices have at once dissolved the borders between our bodies and fortified our singular force fields. I'm a glistening mess of sweat-streaked silver—an unfurled runway, my voice hoarse from shrieking against the lift-off. Every neuron crackling with new transmissions, every pore open and soaked until the whole of my body is one undulating O like that moment in the climax of the song "You Turn Me On," when Patti's voice comes unmoored from her chorus harmonies with Nona and Sarah—*It's good whatcha doin' whatcha doin' / It's good watcha Oooohhhh*—and becomes an unleashed tripling pulse of fulfillment: a river of *Ouh-oh-Uh*'s coursing out past the song's end.

I make my way toward the bathroom to reshape the angles of my crumpled cardboard Aztec pyramid crown and all around me are folks spilling in and out of the stalls, relinquishing themselves to the body's wants. Some snort and others suck. Some preen and others push. Some share what they've got and others close their mouths together in a sealed lock. All of us glistening and alive with desire and our shared movements toward satiety. Someone with a swaggering silver-smeared body is bent over before me and is asking for help buffing up the faded silver sheen on their upturned ass and soon I'm lathering on silvery cream and rubbing and polishing until it returns to its glow as a shimmering moon. *It's good whatcha doin' whatcha doin'*. Everyone is an unlatched portal, blossoming orifice and dizzying precipice, all pursed lips and flicked fingers and rouged nipples and crack and lobe and slit and ooze and drip and spurt, all earthly delight even as our silvery souls unsheathe themselves and ascend from the body's hold.

The next act, "Nightbirds," begins with a singular and pure-note hum rippling through the darkness. There's a light caress of drums before the wavering *mmmmms* evolve into words, *Nightbird fly by the light of the moon*, and the faintest glow of light begins to frame the preening, black-feathered silhouette of Sarah center stage as she holds the note as effortlessly as a chalice holds wine. We are all on our feet, hushed with anticipation and reverence. Nona's bass tone rides in under Sarah's high call as Nona strides out like an intergalactic white peacock with its

Labelle in concert

plumes fully spread. We are riveted, alert in shared awareness
of a shift from matter to spirit, or rather the presence of the
spirit latent in and unleashed from the material world.

And then the sky cracks open.

Down comes a fluttering cascade of feathers and fur trailing for yards and yards, a black and orange meteor-blur, a
trailing flame and its smoldering wake. It's Patti descending
from the flies with an avian wail. The three voices swooping
and soaring and embroidering the sky with their formations,
a bird-song flitting back and forth from ethereal trill to low
hover. A song of spirit and matter and the shattering of the
space between them. *It's a nightbird's way.*

Before us not just a trinity of divas but a diva-trinity—
human animal goddess—spectral terrestrial alien—an oblit-

eration of binaries and the triangulated hierarchies of lead singer-and-her-backups—the crescendo of power shifted and toppled and redesigned—and all of us pressing closer together, Labelle showing us how to be in relation to each other, to the others, in the forsaken city.

By the time we hear that outstretched organ note— unfurled skybridge, just-in-time exit ramp—that launches "Lady Marmalade," there's no divide we haven't crossed, there's no one and nothing we haven't touched. Moved so completely and purely toward one another until, as Whitman wrote to his passing stranger, *your body has become not yours only nor left my body mine only.* Here in the steady four-on-the-floor propulsion of drums and horns and in the summoning, *Hey sister, go sister, soul sister,* our true names are called, our voices are heard, our bodies are ours at last. We are melding together singing and shrieking and shimmying and opening ourselves wide until we are the *savage beast inside,* until we are our own Eves convulsing with the ecstasy of knowing, of being known in and through our dance-anthem and the way it moves and moves and moves us. The way it delights in *Marmalade* and all that is sweet and sticky and flowing from our sated bodies.

We dance our way out, all the way out until we reach the basalt-powdered surface of the moon and out even farther toward the obsidian stillness on its other side.

Labelle lands us as they often do with a question, *Have you got a minute, my friend?* Their songs are filled with questions, all of them propelled by a desire for intimate and honest relations: *Are you lonely? Space children, are there any others? Why don't you come outside and play and stay, stay with me?*

Have you got a minute, my friend? They ask, launching the second act's closing song, "(Can I Speak to You Before You Go to) Hollywood?" It begins with Nona offering advice to Sarah, playing the role of a concerned friend warning against the isolating dangers of becoming a cog churning through Hollywood's star-making machinery. She reaches out for one last moment of candid connection before departure. And just when we think these are their assigned roles, Sarah is echoing Nona's advice back to her and just when we think they will sing a duet, Patti approaches and takes over, repeating and revising the role of wise counselor, all of them together defying the lyrics that suggest a perspective directed from a singular I to a singular you. They are singing to one another and to all of us, none of us immune to Hollywood's allure: it could be you or you or me or you.

And just when we think they're singing only about the dangers of Hollywood, Sarah stretches out the word "end" in delicate melisma and then takes a brief breath before finishing her question in the final verse. The pause after "the end" barely perceptible but registering loud and clear. Labelle insists we consider the end, the inevitability of departure, of loss, of the end-days. Listen to their melded voices. Can you hear how they are showing us how to embrace one another in our swaying and our singing? Let's hold ourselves so close that our voices pulse through each other's sinews and marrow and every searching vein.

There's no singular with Labelle. No sealed binary in the duet. No hierarchical triangulation. They are a diva trio, after all. And so the song moves from light accompaniment and solitary voices to a crescendo of vibes and percussion and skyrocketing harmonies. In the final moments of the song, they expand the you of their chorus and expand the you of our consciousness as they repeat and revise, *Oh I, I believe in you and you and you and you and you. . . .*

Let's hold onto every *you*, in the knowledge that we may not have long left. Because when are dark girls ever sure of their chances for a tomorrow except perhaps when we are held deep inside of a song? So you and I reach for one another within the flock of Labelle's migratory voices, within their insistence on the relational ethos of you and you and you and you. What else is there to do in a city of ash and plague when you know that soon you'll be gone on your way?

But before we part we are a constellation of delirious applause and testifying praise, an ovation for the ages, a meteor shower of worship and gratitude and fulfillment. And the divas respond by riding down the celestial trails of our adulation, touching down for their encore. Labelle shake themselves loose from the stage, shaking tambourines and hips and brass horns and shoulders and drum sticks and the floor beneath us all. They join us in the aisles and we all dance together to their closing question, *What Can I Do for You?*, the title of our favorite dance-floor groove. The unleashed rhythms—guitar riffs and tripleting horns—and endless permutations of vocal patterns—spiraling solos and grounded unison and expansive harmonies and dizzying descant—expand the dimensions of the song until it's big enough to hold us all. Who else could create a song-space capacious enough to fit us all in along with our abundant yearnings and struggles and with room left to dance?

It's all here in the lyrics: war and peace and truth and nothingness and rain and light and happiness and confusion. And we are, all of us, in here—you and I and all our sisters and brothers—doing all of the things we do—living and suffering and needing and hating and, of course, loving and loving and loving. Who else could pull it off, could put it all in—all those abstract nouns and all of the well-trodden verbs—without contracting into cliché? Who else but Labelle could carry it off, could carry us through and leave us asking *What can I do for you?* and asking back, *What can you do for me?* over and over and over and over in a funk-ass, open-ended, disco-drive, in its insistent refusal of closure? We're fifteen minutes into this encore number but what's time to space girls like us who've found our home in the unfolding beat and unanswered questions of the song?

Labelle is dancing with us in the aisles and we orbit one another, the centripetal force of our shared desire drawing us closer and closer, all of us in deep relation to one another across the vast expanse of the shattered city, until, like neutron stars, we can't help but collide, our collision creating a ripple in the fabric of space-time, our fusion (so the scientists say) the very source of all those precious metals—the gold of ancient Egypt and the platinum of jet engines roaring across the sky and, yes, something silver. The silver of loose change and crowned teeth and the Boscoreale Treasure. The silver streaks in my aging hair and the silver earrings swaying from your ears as we hold each other close and spin together farther and farther out. The silver of chrome rims and streetlamps. The silver of ceremony. And all that silver gleaming from the blasted shafts of the city broken open by our wounds and our wants.

Can you feel us blasting off, hurtling back to the future once more? Can you hear Labelle's voices guiding our return? Hear the signals they are sending through the portable speaker in the room we now share? Stay awhile. Let's hit repeat. Let's listen together to the sound of their union. The shared leads, the varied and virtuosic vocal meldings. What can I do for you? What can you do for me? It's the sound of mutual aid. The sound of the young woman on Frederick Douglass Boulevard handing out water to the protesters, the sound of the car revving up and loaded with a girl who needs to cross state lines for an abortion, the sound of a house party thrown to raise money for another girl's top surgery, the sound of the door opening to shelter the weary migrant. The sound of community care, of fugitive arrangements, of flight beyond established octaves and enclaves. The sound of the lonely-no-more and the no-longer-strangers and all the space children. The sound we follow to find each other in and beyond the city we call home.

Lucia's Last Act

My first theatrical outing when the theatres reopened after the pandemic lockdown was to the Metropolitan Opera for a production of *Lucia di Lammermoor* featuring Latina diva Nadine Sierra in the title role. I had scored three complimentary tickets and had invited two of my girlfriends—fellow writers who've been steady companions on this diva journey—to join me. I figured what better way to celebrate a diva's return than with other remarkable women I cherished.

Despite my years spent worshipping divas in New York City, I had never been to the Met for an opera. The spring I lived in Paris, I had been fortunate enough to attend the 2014 staging of *The Magic Flute* at the Opéra Bastille. My companion that evening was a colleague from the Sorbonne who wore a pair of silvery-gray jeans and the most exquisitely, effortlessly draped Hermès scarf. I learned that night the true meaning of élan. And how a diva's voice can transcend the confines of a misogynist libretto.

In the week leading up to my first night at the Met, I felt a little like Cher in *Moonstruck*, worrying over what to wear and dyeing the gray out of my hair. As for Nadine Sierra, despite her young age (a mere 33 years old), *Lucia* was not her Met debut. Often referred to as a child prodigy, Sierra, at age 20, was the youngest singer ever to win the Metropolitan Opera's vocal competition that crowns promising young opera singers. She went on to perform in opera houses all over the world. This was her third go at *Lucia* that year, having sung the role in Naples and Munich before New York. Divas-to-be like Nadine Sierra show us how to make an entrance. Indeed, they often achieve their diva-ness through the flawless execution of an awe-inspiring arrival.

Lucia di Lammermoor is a romantic opera by Italian composer Gaetano Donizetti that premiered in Naples in 1835. Loosely based upon Sir Walter Scott's 1819 historical novel *The Bride of Lammermoor*, Donizetti's version is one of the most famous examples of *bel canto* opera known, as the name suggests, for emphasizing the beauty and technique of its singers in their delivery of its florid phrasings. Set in the hills of eighteenth-century Scotland, the plot follows the travails of Lucia, whose love for Edgardo is thwarted by her brother (Enrico), who demands that she marry another man (Arturo) to secure the family's standing and power. In response to Enrico's insistence that the marriage bed awaits her, Lucia replies, *The tomb, the tomb awaits me!* In the second act, Lucia reluctantly marries Arturo after being tricked by her brother into believing that Edgardo has betrayed her. When she signs the marriage certificate, she cries out, *I have signed my death-warrant.* As for most opera diva characters, marriage for Lucia is a death trap. In the final act, she emerges from the wedding chamber, having murdered Arturo, her white dress splattered with his blood. She then proceeds to sing "Il dolce suono" (The Sweet Sound), one of the most gravity-defying arias in all of opera, in which she imagines herself reunited with Edgardo before she fatally succumbs to her madness. She has lost her mind to grief. Murder and madness are the only paths she can forge away from her life as transactional property in the patriarchal order.

In the production that I saw in spring 2022, director Simon Stone brilliantly transported the setting from the eighteenth-century Scottish highlands to the late twentieth-century ruins of a Rust Belt town devastated by economic decline and the opioid crisis. The remains of the town rotated on a revolving set: the blinkered neon signs of a pawnshop and a cheap motel, the fluorescent glare of a pharmacy and a liquor store. The set was framed by screens that alternated close-up shots of the performers (shot live by camera crews trailing the actors) with scrolling text messages, Facebook posts, and cell phone photos foregrounding the proliferation of screen culture and its pervasiveness in the public and private realms of modern life. The result, which I found astonishing, was both an intimate portrait of Lucia and a large-scale rendering of the grand scope of her woe. In this world, Lucia is a recovering addict, Edgardo is shipped off to fight in the Persian Gulf, and Arturo dies when Lucia strikes him with a fire extinguisher in their seedy motel room. A world saturated with desperate longing and few escape routes.

Sierra's Lucia moved through the blasted urban landscape in torn jeans, a sequined tank top, hoop earrings, and a cropped pink puffer jacket; her wedding gown was an all-American dollop of satin and puffed sleeves and embroidered sweetheart collar and piles of tulle. In other words, the costume of a contemporary diva. Her eyes flashed with coquettish delight, her expressions drawn with so much want. Watching her was like watching a campfire crackle and spark into a forest fire, like watching the trees stripped and still smoking from the blaze.

The role of Lucia is famous for the demands it places on the divas who inhabit the role, in particular, for the 15-minute-long "mad scene" in Act III that requires literal breathtaking endurance from its coloratura soprano, who must not only reach her signature dramatic heights but also sing across a wide range. She must scale the mountains and swim the seas. Reflecting on performing Lucia's final aria, French diva Natalie Dessay once said, *I used to like to challenge myself. . . And see to what point I could go—with the risk of falling down, of course.*

The aria unfastens Lucia's tethers to this bleak world through a duet traditionally sung with the flute or, as in the Met's production, with the glass harmonica played by Friedrich Heinrich Kern in an extended cadenza. The alternations of intense ornamentation and the tremulous ascent of her voice knock everything off its bearings, her embellishments delicately placing pieces of fine crystal in a China cabinet only to topple it over, covering everything around her in shards of glass. In his review of Sierra's performance for the *Washington Post*, Michael Andor Brodeur wrote, *She ornamented her final aria as though blithely decorating a dead tree.* That night at the Met, I sat by that ornamented tree and received the gifts Sierra laid out before it. That night, she made her entrance into my diva pantheon.

After Lucia's aria, Edgardo discovers the news about Lucia and kills himself. But for me what came after her final song seemed simply like annotation. The diva was done. All I remember hearing after the end of her aria is the chorus singing, *The world is empty without Lucia.*

Oh, how I miss Lucia. My Lucia. My Tía. My first and forever diva. My fistful of dollars. My silver bullet. My up the ante. Her brain now pocked by the ravages of Alzheimer's disease. Her fighting spirit now a dying ember. *Lucia is gone*, the chorus sings. Tía's last letters to me and the diary entries she recorded just before entering the memory ward of the Buena Vida nursing home showed the early signs of her tremulous descent. *Started writing in this book. Wondering what is happening to me.—It is now 8:20pm?? It's dark outside. Phone is dead. 9pm—I really think I need to start taking my memory pills again.*

Like Sierra's Lucia di Lammermoor, Tía Lucia endured patriarchal violence and economic hardships in a world that often deemed her crazy or too much. *I know what it is to be "abused" by a man*, she once wrote to me in a letter chronicling the O. J. Simpson trial. And like the divas who take on the role of Lucia, Tía performed with astonishing flair through the suffering. Once, in response to an invitation she received when she was sick, Tía wrote, *He wanted to know if I was going to the party on Sunday. I said yes—<u>cough & all</u>.*

Tía, like the character Lucia, saw marriage as a trap. She simply refused to contract herself into the role. Not for the Turkish lover who wanted to whisk her far away from home. Not for any of the neighborhood boys. Not for the ones who had stolen her heart or her money or both. Certainly not for the ones who raised a hand to her. Not even that time she got all dressed up and tagged along to the Renaissance Festival and a costumed duke knelt before her on the matted weeds offering his hand, pleading for hers. Not even then. Instead she waved a twenty at him and said, *Oh please, I don't need a man, what I need is another turkey leg.* Not even after he fetched it for her and returned to his knees. Instead, she wandered off, smoked turkey leg in her hand like a scepter, and made her way toward the royal procession.

Opera afficionados have long delighted in the pleasurable (punishing? pleasurably punishing?) tension built into the heart of the genre: a supernaturally powerful diva performer sings the role of a diva character who invariably suffers a catastrophic fate, her virtuosic singing simultaneously transcending and trapped by the circumstances of plot. Carmen is stabbed by Don José as they sing the duet "C'est toi? C'est moi!" In *La Bohème*, Mimí, coughing violently, still manages to sing a duet with her great love, the poet Rodolfo, before succumbing to tuberculosis. Violetta sings a duet with her reunited lover, Alfredo, on her deathbed in *La Traviata*, before succumbing to—yes—tuberculosis. Norma is sentenced to death by fire for her witchy priestess ways. Tosca flings herself off the battlement to her death. And in her final aria, Lucia goes mad—scaling registers and unfurling coloraturas—imagining a reunion with her lover, Edgardo, before—more trills and leaps—she dies. *Carmen dies*, Susan Leonardi and Rebecca Pope write, *but, oh, her arias!*

Divas, opera reminds us, are linked with death, with spectacular, blood-soaked, chest-rattling, grief-stricken, falling-from-great-heights, stretched-out-over-impossibly-

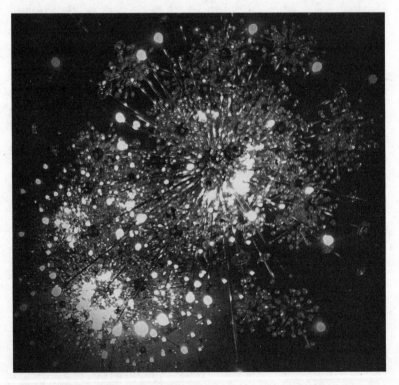

Sparkling chandelier at the Met

high-notes-and-coughing-bouts death. And, as Lucia's final aria demonstrates, divas are known as well for their capacity for endurance against all odds. Opera insists that the life and death of a complicated, virtuosic, larger-than-life woman are worthy of tragedy on an epic scale. Opera's very structure builds toward a climax that demands we linger on the final moments of a diva's life.

Like the grandest of opera diva characters, Tía Lucia made an aria out of her everyday moments of aspiration and sorrow, and she faced the twilight of her days on her own. On her own terms. With a diva's devastating lyric flourish.

Light is very dim in Living
Room. Phone is dead.

Tía's exquisite voice, preserved in her letters, reminds me that as much as divas teach us about making an entrance, they also teach us how to make an exit. In one of her last letters to me, Tía Lucia wrote with delight and solemnity, her words both ode and elegy: *Debbie, you should have seen the Eclipse. When I first saw it, I thought I was dreaming. . . . It was beautiful. Like a big shining star moving very slowly. Light was shining around it until it was covered up completely.*

Acknowledgments

This book was over a decade in the making. But in many ways, it really began at a Baskin-Robbins in San Antonio, Texas, sometime in the late 1970s on one of my regular outings with Tía Lucia Bustillo. She ordered the Matterhorn (a now long-discontinued specialty) which was the biggest sundae on the menu—seven scoops, five toppings—and let me pick out all the flavors. We scaled that mountain of cascading sweetness, one savored spoonful after another, until we finished it off. Then we went to dinner. Thank you, Tía, for teaching me that more is more and that pleasure is a birthright and that a brown girl could grow up to be grand and messy and sharp and unruly and fabulous and deserving of love and adoration.

My critical and devotional approach to divas blossomed in conversations and collaborations with the profoundly visionary artist Daniel Alexander Jones that we started in poorly lit basement offices at University of Texas–Austin and on long stretches of Texas-highway car rides in 2004 and have continued across the country and across the years. Daniel, thank you and your alter(altar)-ego, Jomama Jones, for inspiring me and expanding my diva repertoire ever since.

Nicole Dewey was an early and ardent champion of this book and is an incisive reader and the most devoted friend.

Here's to the next thirty-five years of busted flats in Baton Rouge and book talks in NYC.

Enormous thanks to my agent Sarah Burnes and my editor Amy Cherry for believing in this project and for offering insights that made this a better book. Thank you to the Norton team for their talents and expertise: Huneeya Siddiqui, Jodi Beder, and all those who contributed to the book's design and marketing.

Thank you to everyone who answered my diva-related questions and whose insights or experiences inform or make appearances in my writing. My thanks to Lisa Jones Brown, Moira Hodgson, Colleen McGinley Pence, and all the members of the circle: Michelle Boyd, Regina Deil-Amen, Heather McClure, and Gina Pérez.

I am grateful to all the wonderful research assistants at UT–Austin and Columbia University who followed every diva lead. Thank you to Nicole Gurgel, Faith Andrews, Laura Lewin, Juliana DeVaan, Beca Baca, Aleena Garrison, Elianna Lee, and Isabella Ramírez. Thanks especially to Elianna for extensive research on diva girlhood and Isabella for heroic work on licensing and permissions.

I cannot heap enough praise on the extraordinary Alondra Nelson, whose brilliance is matched by her generosity. During her time as the dean of Social Sciences at Columbia University, she provided steadfast support and crucial funding for early research on this project. Thanks as well to Dean Sarah Cole and the Office of the Executive Vice President for Arts and Sciences for awarding this project a Lenfest Junior Faculty Development Grant to cover image rights and licensing fees.

I had the great fortune to write, revise, and think through several of these chapters during residencies at the Blue Mountain Center and the American Academy in Rome. Thank you to all who labored to keep me creatively inspired and well fed during my stays. I'm deeply grateful as well to Jill Dolan, Stacy

Wolf, Dolores Inés Casillas, Eva Woods Peiró, and Michelle Boyd, who opened up their homes or joined me on long weekends for our own DIY writing retreats.

Thank you to everyone who invited me to present my work on divas and provided valuable feedback on the ideas I shared: Margo Crawford and Mary Pat Brady at Cornell University; Vikki Bell at Goldsmiths, University of London; Liza Gennaro at Manhattan School of Music; Stacy Wolf, Jill Dolan, and Dick Hartog at Princeton University; Nadine George-Graves at Northwestern University; Marcia Sells at the Met Opera; Carina Olaru at Purdue University; and Francesca Royster, Oliver Wang, and Eric Weisbard at the Popular Music Books in Process series. Thanks as well to the editors who published earlier versions of some of the material from this book: Lourdes Torres at *Latino Studies Journal*, Soham Patel at *The Georgia Review*, and Ann Powers at *NPR Music*.

My thinking and writing about divas has benefitted tremendously from colleagues in music, dance, and performance studies and from fellow diva devotees. Clare Croft and Anthea Kraut shared their brilliant dance scholar insights; Leonard Nevarez, Karl Hagstrom-Miller, and Lee Edwards shared their expertise as musicians and music scholars; Jack Isaac Pryor shared their reliably astute insights as a performance studies scholar; Ricardo Abreu Bracho read with an exacting editorial eye and offered generous feedback on an early version of the book. Margo Jefferson and Lynn Melnick generously read my work and shared a deep love for writing in praise of divas. Thanks as well to Morgan Blue, Dolores Inés Casillas, Diana Delgado, Farah Jasmine Griffin, Amy Hagstrom-Miller, Jack Halberstam, Shirley Thompson Marshall, Lisa Moore, Lisa Olstein, Shana Redmond, Cherise Smith, Deb Vargas, and Kristen Warner.

I am fortunate to be surrounded by talented colleagues at Columbia whose writing and friendship sustains me: Margo

Jefferson, Wendy Walters, Timothy Donnelly, Dorothea Lasky, Lynn Xu, Heidi Julavits, Lis Harris, Victor LaValle, Marie Lee, Sayantani Dasgupta, Mae Ngai, Karl Jacoby, George Chauncey, Ron Gregg, and Meehan Crist.

I have been immensely inspired by the students in my diva seminars over the years at UT–Austin and Columbia. Thank you for deepening my understanding of what a diva is and what she makes possible for those of us who are devoted to her.

Abundant thanks to my cherished friends and collaborators in New York City who have nurtured me and my work: Rhonda Braxton, Chris Brown, Arielle Cribb, Arlene Davila, Mary Gannon, Aracelis Girmay, Macarena Gómez-Barris, Saidiya Hartman, Joseph Legaspi, Ricky Maldonado, Lynn Melnick, Lien-Hang Nguyen, Urayoán Noel, Judy Polyne, Millery Polyne, Neferti Tadiar, the Bank Street School community, and everyone who drops by for Thirsty Thursdays. I'm especially and eternally grateful to Angie Cruz & Sarah Gambito for the magic they regularly make that lights my creative path and sustains my emotional well-being.

Thank you to Elizabeth Emens, Georgia Lee, and Michelle Boyd for showing up every week with intention and integrity. Michelle, thanks for holding everything I've showed up with over the years.

I am deeply grateful to my family, who have cheered on all of my writerly endeavors. Mil gracias to my parents Gilberto and Consuelo Villarreal, my Bronx parents Francisco and Amparo Guridy, my diva *prima* Marisela Salinas and my soul-sisters Celeste Guzmán Mendoza, Michele Archange, and Eva Woods Peiró (especially, Eva, for our epic retreats).

Profound thanks to Stacy Wolf—dear friend, stellar writing-duet partner, and longtime diva-collaborator—who offered careful readings, thoughtful feedback, clarifying dialogue, and unwavering encouragement of this project from its earliest, roughest drafts. My writing about performance is indelibly shaped and sharpened by your work and by our generative conversations about all the divas we love.

Macarena Gómez-Barris and Saidiya Hartman read multiple drafts of this book more than once and responded with rigor and radical love. Maca insisted that *the heart of your book is there; don't break it.* Saidiya insisted on more blood, sweat, and tears, which is to say, more risk on every page. Your minds are as expansive as your hearts—big enough to hold me and my work accountable to the highest standards. I'm eternally grateful for all the ways each of you heard my true voice and helped me channel it into a more honest book.

My dear daughter Zaya, thank you for indulging my outsized appetites for all things overmuch and for patiently distracting yourself with another episode of the latest Korean drama while I wrote well into the night. I can't wait to play more spades with you and watch more tennis together and cheer on even more of your impressive feats at first base now that this book is finally done.

This book would not have been possible without the emotional support and editorial eye of my beloved Frank Andre Guridy. The love, admiration, and gratitude I have for you is boundless. Even as you were facing down your own book deadline, you always took the time to talk through ideas, proofread countless drafts, and delight in diva performances with me. Among my favorite moments was our shared awe as we witnessed Cynthia Erivo perform the role of Celie in the 2015 revival of *The Color Purple.* As Celie sings in the closing number, *your heartbeat / make my heart beat.*

Notes

PROLOGUE

3   *the best girl singer*: Margaret Wappler, "Vikki Carr," *Los Angeles Times*, 16 July 2010, https://projects.latimes.com/hollywood/star-walk/vikki-carr/index.html.

3   *"I can only work with one diva"*: Gary James, "Gary James Interviews Vikki Carr," n.d., http://www.classicbands.com/VikkiCarrInterview.html.

DIVA DEFINITIONS

8   *We shall love each other*: Audre Lorde, "Martha," *Cables to Rage* (London: Paul Breman, 1970), 10.

9   *the squint-eyed*: Gloria Anzaldúa, *Borderlands/La Frontera: The New Mestiza* (San Francisco: Aunt Lute Press, 1987), 25.

11   *It made me look hard*: Grace Jones, *I'll Never Write My Memoirs* (New York: Gallery Books, 2015), 81.

12   *I was born*: Jones, *I'll Never Write My Memoirs*, 1.

12   *The diva hasn't yet arrived at herself*: Wayne Koestenbaum, *The Queen's Throat: Opera, Homosexuality, and the Mystery of Desire* (New York: Poseidon Press [Re-printed by Da Capo Press, 2001]), 86.

12   *I am always becoming something*: Jones, *I'll Never Write My Memoirs*, 380.

13   *I looked natural and unnatural*: Jones, *I'll Never Write My Memoirs*, 120.

13   *I am rooted and restless*: Jones, *I'll Never Write My Memoirs*, xiii.

13   *My shaved head made me look more abstract*: Jones, *I'll Never Write My Memoirs*, 82.

14   **Because of this gender blurring:** Diva scholars Susan Leonardi and Rebecca Pope describe how these tensions make the diva *ever a gender disorder*. Susan Leonardi and Rebecca Pope, *The Diva's Mouth: Body, Voice, Prima Donna Politics* (New Brunswick, NJ: Rutgers University Press, 1996), 163. Film scholar Brett Farmer writes about the life-sustaining *insistently queer pleasures* that

gay male diva worship offers. Brett Farmer, "The Fabulous Sublimity of Gay Diva Worship," *Camera Obscura* 59 20.22 (2005): 169. Feminist theatre critic Stacy Wolf delights in Broadway divas *as sources of pleasure and power for feminist and lesbian spectators.* Stacy Wolf, *A Problem Like Maria: Gender and Sexuality in the American Musical* (Ann Arbor: University of Michigan Press, 2002), viii.

14   *I recognized in her thrilling contrariness*: Francesca Royster, *Sounding Like a No-No: Queer Sounds and Eccentric Acts in the Post-Soul Era* (Ann Arbor: University of Michigan Press, 2012), 150.

14   *A diva is said to* come out: Koestenbaum, *The Queen's Throat*, 86.

14   *My life . . . is out there*: Jones, *I'll Never Write My Memoirs*, ix.

14   *a frenzied fantasy world*: Jones, *I'll Never Write My Memoirs*, 164.

16   *Shaving my head*: Jones, *I'll Never Write My Memoirs*, 82.

16   *I was preaching pleasure*: Jones, *I'll Never Write My Memoirs*, 258.

17   *In my own way*: Jones, *I'll Never Write My Memoirs*, 24.

17   *My instincts were to become*: Jones, *I'll Never Write My Memoirs*, 52.

18   *I am in three or four time zones*: Jones, *I'll Never Write My Memoirs*, 281.

18   *a witch with a smear of blood*: Jones, *I'll Never Write My Memoirs*, 128.

19   *Black women's singing*: Farah Jasmine Griffin, "When Malindy Sings: A Meditation on Black Women's Vocality," *In Search of a Beautiful Freedom: New and Selected Essays* (New York: W.W. Norton & Co., 2023), 38.

19   *many registers*: Daphne Brooks, *Liner Notes for the Revolution: The Intellectual Life of Black Feminist Sound* (Cambridge MA: The Belknap Press of Harvard University Press, 2021), 2.

19   *has a loud voice*: Leonardi and Pope, *The Diva's Mouth*, 19.

19   *In a funny way*: Matthew Epstein qtd. in Will Crutchfield, "There Are Singers and Then There Are Divas," *New York Times*, 26 Jan 1986.

20   *What can we learn from women*: Angela Davis, *Blues Legacies and Black Feminism: Gertrude Ma Rainey, Bessie Smith and Billie Holiday* (New York: Vintage Books, 1998), xi. Other foundational works that turn to Black divas in their explorations of Black feminism include Hazel Carby, "It Just Be's Dat Way Sometime: The Sexual Politics of Women's Blues," in *Unequal Sisters: A Multicultural Reader in U.S. Women's History*, ed. Ellen Carol DuBois and Vicki Ruiz (New York: Routledge, 1990), 238–49; Farah Jasmine Griffin, *If You Can't Be Free, Be a Mystery: In Search of Billie Holiday* (New York: Free Press, 2001); Daphne Duval Harrison, *Black Pearls: Blues Queens of the 1920s* (New Brunswick, NJ: Rutgers University Press, 1988); Hortense Spillers, "Interstices: A Small Drama of Words," in *Black, White, and in Color: Essays on American Literature and Culture* (Chicago: University of Chicago Press, 2003), 152–75.

20   *sexuality is not privatized*: Angela Davis, *Blues Legacies and Black Feminism*, 91.

21   *She showed me the air*: Janis Joplin, in "Bessie Smith: Empress of the Blues," http://www.janisjoplin.net/music/influences/bessie-smith/.

21   *Is you in school?*: Chris Albertson, *Bessie* (New Haven: Yale University Press, 2005), 230.

24   *We have the deep throats*: Jones, *I'll Never Write My Memoirs*, 256.

25   *These days, you can't throw*: Andrew Essex, "Viva las Divas," *Entertainment Weekly*. 9 Oct 1998, 32.

26   *I hate that word diva*: Jones, *I'll Never Write My Memoirs*, 377.
29   *When I retire*: Jones, *I'll Never Write My Memoirs*, 369.

DIVA STYLE

30   *delightful naughtiness*: Grace Jones, *I'll Never Write My Memoirs* (New York: Gallery Books, 2015), 36.
30   *My appreciation of what an Auntie is*: Wesley Morris, *Still Processing*, "We Love Aunties," *New York Times*, 22 Mar 2018, https://podcasts.apple.com/lt/podcast/we-love-aunties/id1151436460?i=1000407134869.
31   *Well, guess who*: All letter excerpts in this chapter are from my own personal collection of letters sent to me from my Tía Lucia Bustillo from 1993 to 2003.

DIVA MOVIDAS

41   *Why do we all have to be the same color?*: Rita Moreno, *Life without Makeup*, David Galligan, dir., Berkeley Repertory Theatre, October 2011.
43   *I never wanted to be that wimpy Maria*: Jennifer Lopez, *"West Side Story* Revisited,"   http://www.vanityfair.com/culture/features/2009/03/west-side-story-portfolio200903.
49   *Look! Instead of a shampoo*: *West Side Story*, dir. Jerome Robbins and Robert Wise, dir.; Ernest Lehman, screenplay; Natalie Wood, George Chakiris, Rita Moreno, perf. (MGM, 1961; DVD, MGM, 2003). All quotes from the musical are from this film version. In the stage version, "America" was choreographed as an argument among the Shark women, but for the film, lyricist Sondheim transformed the number into a debate between the male and female Sharks. The men long for their island home and condemn the structures of racism that mark their lives in New York City. The women defend the possibilities offered by the shining machinery—the washing machines and skyscrapers and Cadillacs—of the mainland U.S. While in many ways the scene enacts long-standing arguments among Puerto Ricans about their fraught status in the U.S. as both citizens and colonial subjects, the film's reassigned lyrics portray the men as incisive critics and the women as deluded consumers.
52   *right to be different*: Renato Rosaldo, "Cultural Citizenship and Educational Democracy," *Cultural Anthropology*, 9.3 (1994): 409.
53   *being singular plural*: José Esteban Muñoz, *Cruising Utopia: The There and Then of Queer Futurity* (New York: New York University Press, 2009), 15.
54   *A brown commons . . . systemic harm*: José Esteban Muñoz, *The Sense of Brown* (Durham, NC: Duke University Press, 2020), 7, 4.
55   **Through the course of their intimate duet**: Stacy Wolf classifies this song as a *queer pedagogical duet* in "'We'll Always Be Bosom Buddies': Female Duets and the Queering of Broadway Musical Theater," *GLQ: A Journal of Lesbian and Gay Studies* 12.3 (2006): 351–76.
57   *Anita was the only Hispanic character*: Rita Moreno interviewed by Michael Schulman, "Rita Moreno Has Time Only for the Truth," *New Yorker*, 17 June 2021, https://www.newyorker.com/culture/the-new-yorker-interview/rita-moreno-has-time-only-for-the-truth.

DIVA COMEBACK

61 *I was still in the Army Reserve*: John Fogerty qtd. in Marc Meyers, *Anatomy of a Song: The Oral History of 45 Iconic Hits that Changed Rock, R&B, and Pop* (New York: Grove Press, 2016).

61 *We made that song our own*: Tina Turner with Kurt Loder, *I, Tina: My Life Story* (New York: Icon It! Books, 1986), 160.

64 *Tina Turner's "roughness"*: Francesca Royster, "Nice and Rough: The Promise of Privacy in Tina Turner's 'What's Love Got To Do With It' and *I, Tina*," *Performance Research: A Journal of the Performing Arts* 12.3 (2007): 107.

65 *I was / so utterly bereft*: Rafael Campo, "Diva," in *Diva* (Durham, NC: Duke University Press, 1999), 33.

66 *quotable . . . fierce labor*: Madison Moore, "Tina Theory: Notes on Fierceness," *Journal of Popular Music Studies* 24.1 (2012): 84.

67 *playfully outrageous*: Royster, "Nice and Rough": 112.

67 *fierceness as a spastic bodily possession*: Moore, "Tina Theory," 83.

68 *Do y'all make up . . . throw it together*: *Soul Train*, 22 April 1972, Season 1, Episode 30, Don Cornelius Productions.

68 *freedom*: Tina Turner interviewed by Laura Schreffler, "Tina Turner: 'How I Found Joy against the Odds,'" *Haute Living*, 1 Dec 2020, https://hauteliving.com/2020/12/tina-turner-shares-how-she-beat-the-odds-to-find-happiness/692384/.

70 *I was afraid*: Tina Turner interview in the documentary *Tina*, Dan Lindsay & T. J. Martin, dir., HBO Films, 2021. Details of the account of the night Tina left Ike at the Hilton Hotel in Dallas are drawn from the documentary and Tina's autobiography, *I, Tina*.

71 *I was running by then*: Turner, *I, Tina*, 190.

71 *That is when I realized*: Turner interview in the documentary, *Tina*.

71 *I moved junk*: Turner, *I, Tina*, 194.

72 *But you and I know there's more to life*: *Ann-Margret Olsson* (variety show), Dwight Hemion, dir., 23 Jan 1975.

73 *By the mid-1970s, diva duets*: Kelly Kessler writes about diva performances on variety shows during this era in *Broadway in the Box: Television's Lasting Love Affair with the Musical* (New York: Oxford University Press, 2020).

73 *She was having trouble with Ike*: Ann-Margret qtd. in George Hamilton, "Ann-Margret," *Interview*, 10 July 2014, https://www.interviewmagazine.com/culture/ann-margret.

75 *When she discovers her diva-incipience*: Koestenbaum, *The Queen's Throat*, 87.

75 *And then I thought, I'm gonna have to dance*: "Legendary Duet," 30 May 2008, https://www.oprah.com/oprahshow/legendary-duet_1/all.

76 *Tina Turner: the woman who taught Mick Jagger*: *People Weekly*, 7 Dec 1981.

77 *I don't consider it a comeback album*: Turner interview in the documentary, *Tina*.

77 *I'm not so thrilled*: Turner interview in the documentary, *Tina*.

78 *First you must get the story*: Grey Eagle Ken Jackson, quoted by his partner, Anne Huggins, in a conversation we shared about the traumas of war at Hedgebrook, Whidbey Island, WA, August 2011.

78 *It's like when soldiers come back*: Erwin Bach interview in the documentary, *Tina*.

78 *All this I built*: *Mad Max Beyond Thunderdome*, George Miller and George
    Ogilvie, dir.; Terry Hayes and George Miller, screenwriters; Mel Gibson, Tina
    Turner, perf. (Warner Brothers, 1985).
80 *Ain't we a pair*: *Mad Max Beyond Thunderdome*.

DIVA MONSTROSITY

82 **Cyclona . . . at Belvedere Park:** Details of the account of Cyclona's debut are
    drawn from Chon Noriega's "Your Art Disgusts Me: Early ASCO, 1971–1975,"
    East of Borneo, 18 Nov 2010, https://eastofborneo.org/articles/your-art-disgusts
    -me-early-asco-1971-75/ and Jennifer Flores Sternad's interview with Robert
    Legorreta in "Cylcona and Early Chicano Performance Art," *GLQ: A Journal
    of Lesbian and Gay Studies* 12.3 (2006): 475–90.
84 *You know who I am*: *Pink Flamingos*, John Waters, dir. and screenplay; Divine,
    David Lochary, Mink Stole, perf. (Dreamland, 1972; DVD, New Line Home
    Entertainment, 2005).
84 *Divine in those days*: John Waters interviewed in *Movies That Shook the World*,
    "Episode 13: *Pink Flamingos*," Jeff Goldblum, narr. (World of Wonder Produc-
    tion Company, AMC, 16 Dec 2005).
86 *a Miss Piggy for the blissfully depraved*: Brad Darrach, "Death Comes to
    a Quiet Man Who Made Drag Queen History as Divine," *People Weekly*, 21
    March 1988.
88 *You can't see what you are. . . . And—and—die!*: *Moonstruck*, Norman Jew-
    ison, dir.; John Patrick Shanley, screenwriter; Cher, Nicolas Cage, perf.
    (MGM, 1987). All quotations from the film are from this version.
88 *The diva's voice may come shadowed*: Koestenbaum, *The Queen's Throat: Opera,
    Homosexuality, and the Mystery of Desire* (New York: Poseidon Press [Re-printed
    by Da Capo Press, 2001]), 103–4.

DIVA FEMINISM

92 **Tickets to the gala:** Details from Aretha Franklin's performance of "I
    Dreamed a Dream" at President Bill Clinton's Inaugural Gala performance
    on January 19, 1993 are drawn from: https://www.dailymotion.com/video/
    x7x22c3.
96 *the best fuckin' singer*: Billy Preston qtd. in David Ritz, *Respect: The Life of
    Aretha Franklin* (New York: Back Bay Books, 2014), 410.
96 *Black people will be free*: Aretha Franklin qtd. in Farah Jasmine Griffin, "Are-
    tha Franklin—Musical Genius, Truth Teller, Freedom Fighter, *The Nation*, 16
    Aug 2018, https://www.thenation.com/article/archive/aretha-franklin-musical
    -genius-truth-teller-freedom-fighter/.
97 *is not necessarily saying . . . yearning for freedom*: Angela Davis interviewed
    by Amy Goodman, *Democracy Now!*, 17 Aug 2018, https://www.democracynow.
    org/2018/8/17/angela_davis_icon_aretha_franklin_will.
97 *Let us now praise . . . this nation's proud history*: Karen Heller, "Divas: Loud,
    Proud, and Fashionable," *Philadelphia Inquirer*, 19 Mar 1993: E1.
97 *Divas are the overhead smash*: Heller, "Divas: Loud, Proud": E1.
99 *The erotic is a measure*: Audre Lorde, "Uses of the Erotic: The Erotic as

Power," *Sister Outsider: Essays and Speeches* (Berkeley, CA: Crossing Press, 1984), 54.

99 *For the erotic is not*: Lorde, "Uses of the Erotic," 55.

101 *Consider this a narrative . . . herself and the world*: Lisa Jones, *Bulletproof Diva: Tales of Race, Sex, and Hair* (New York: Anchor Books, 1995), 3.

102 *A diva needs to hold on*: Elizabeth Alexander, *Diva Studies: A Verse Play, Callaloo* 19.2 (1996): 489.

102 *The diva certainly is and looks fabulous*: Elizabeth Alexander qtd. in Alvin Klein, "Divas in Metaphor, Divas in Crisis, Divas in Life," *New York Times*, 28 Apr 1996: CN17.

103 *If ever a word . . . crossing the street*: Klein, "Divas in Metaphor": CN17.

104 *Why was my grandmother*: Alexander qtd. in Klein, "Divas in Metaphor": CN17.

106 *A firm terrible*: Gertrude Stein, "Sacred Emily," *Writings, 1903–1932* (New York: Library of America, 1998), 387–96.

107 *orange butterflies & aqua sequins*: ntozake shange, *for colored girls who've considered suicide when the rainbow is enuf: a choreopoem* (New York: Macmillan, 1977), 12.

107 *I wonder if Aretha*: In his biography, David Ritz recounts the stories of Franklin's unpaid taxes and bills.

108 *Melancholy do lip sing*: Stein, "Sacred Emily," 387–96.

108 *Rose is a rose*: Stein, "Sacred Emily": 387–96.

108 *The month after Aretha's legendary*: Details from the "Divas Live" performance are drawn from *Divas Live*, Michael A. Simon, dir., Aretha Franklin, Celine Dion, Mariah Carey, perf., 14 Apr 1998 (VH1, DVD, 1998).

110 *And so the divas scramble*: Alexander, 482.

110 *You've Come a Long Way, Diva*: All phrases in the poem, including the title, are drawn from the following articles: Jenice M. Armstrong, "Leave It to Diva," *Philadelphia Daily News*, 19 Jan 1999; Anonymous, "Whitney, Tina and Brandy Sizzle on *Divas Live '99*," *Jet*, 3 May 1999: 58; JD Considine, "Some Divas Are More Divine Than Others," *The Baltimore Sun*, 15 Oct 1998; Andrew Essex, "Viva Las Divas," *Entertainment Weekly*, 9 Oct 1998: 32–35; Tamara Ikenberg, "Deluge of Divas: It Takes Much Less to Be One These Days," *Milwaukee Journal Sentinel*, 24 Oct 1999; Charles Passy, "Doing Divas a Disservice," *Pittsburgh Post-Gazette*, 4 July 1999.

112 *Women see in other women*: Holly Morris, promotional video, *Adventure Divas*, PBS, 1999, https://vimeo.com/98785110.

112 *I rolled the new ethos around . . . jumped out of airplanes*: Holly Morris, "Diva," *Ms.*, June/July 1999: 13.

114 *sing her sighs*: shange, *for colored girls*, 2.

DIVA RELATIONS

118 *a conjunction of Afro-Cuban music*: Frances Aparicio, "*Así Son*: Salsa Music, Female Narratives, and Gender (De)Construction in Puerto Rico," *Daughters of Caliban: Caribbean Women in the Twentieth Century* (Bloomington: University of Indiana Press, 1997), 261.

120 **There's a clip from 1974:** "Celia Cruz Sound Check! – Zaire '74," https://www.youtube.com/watch?v=mX53j-Wfpyg.

126 *I'm a feminist*: La India qtd. in Alisa Valdes-Rodriguez, "Commanding

Respect," *Los Angeles Times*, 9 Apr 2000, https://www.latimes.com/archives/la
-xpm-2000-apr-09-ca-17469-story.html.

127 *is the most crucial component of the dance*: Cindy Garcia, *Salsa Crossings: Dancing Latinidad in Los Angeles* (Durham, NC: Duke University Press, 2013), 7.

130 *Divas required other women as models*: Koestenbaum, *The Queen's Throat*, 99.

131 **Celia's televised concert for PBS:** Details of the performance are drawn from *Celia Cruz and Friends: A Night of Salsa*, Jay Whitsett, dir., Celia Cruz, La India, Tito Puente, perf., 12 May 1999 (PBS, DVD; PBS Home Video, 1999).

132 *In the place where you love*: Yehuda Amichai, "Poems for a Woman," *The Selected Poetry of Yehuda Amichai*, trans. Chana Bloch and Stephen Mitchell (Oakland: University of California Press, 1996), 18.

DIVA GIRLS

135 **Six days later:** Details from the Venus-Serena semifinals match at the 2008 US Open Tennis Tournament are drawn from https://www.youtube.com/watch?v=JyiBpPk97Jg.

136 *People often ask us*: *Venus & Serena: For Real*, pilot episode, "All in the Family," 20 July 2005, ABC Family.

141 *begging for new rackets . . . "It's racism"*: Joel Stein, "Power Game," *Time*, 3 Sep 2001, 54–63.

141 *People criticize me*: Venus Williams qtd. in Stein, "Power Game," 54.

142 *Some of the players have been critical*: Chris Evert qtd. in Sarah Projansky, *Spectacular Girls: Media Fascination and Celebrity Culture* (New York: New York University Press, 2014), 138.

142 **It was a moment marked by a shift**: Projansky, *Spectacular Girls*; Anita Harris, ed., *All About the Girl: Culture, Power, and Identity* (New York: Routledge, 2004); Anita Harris, *Young Women in the Twenty-First Century* (New York: Routledge, 2004).

142 **She seemed suddenly to be everywhere:** All product information collected from JCPenney, Walmart, and Sears catalogues from 2000 through 2010. Rescue Divas Camp: https://rescuedivas.org/. Paul Martin, "I've Had Enough of Diva Girl Groups," *The Mirror*, 19 May 2008, 7.

143 *Today's girls are getting caught up*: Jessica Bennett, "Are We Turning Tweens into 'Generation Diva?'" *Newsweek*, 29 Mar 2009, https://www.newsweek.com/are-we-turning-tweens-generation-diva-76425.

143 **The first decade of the new century:** Projansky, *Spectacular Girls*, 5; Mary Kearney, "Sparkle: Luminosity and Post-Girl Power Media," *Continuum: Journal of Media and Cultural Studies* 29.2 (2015): 263–73.

145 *McDonald's featured the Diva Starz*: https://www.youtube.com/watch?v=SatgQv-0drw.

147 *I don't know what Richard*: Elena Dementieva qtd. in Leighton Ginn, "Looking Back at the Williams Controversy at BNP," 22 Jan 2014, https://www.desertsun.com/story/sports/tennis/bnp/2014/01/22/looking-back-at-the-williams-controversy-at-bnp/4791323/

147 *Wimbledon Fixed?*: "Wimbledon Fixed? The Shocking Story," *National Enquirer*, 27 Mar 2001.

148 *Boost your ego . . . grant one lucky girl her wish*: Head Wear advertisement, *Seventeen*, May 2001, 104; PacSun Sportswear advertisement, *Seventeen*, May 2001, 3.

148 **The morning of the semifinals match:** Details from the events at Indian Wells on March 15–17, 2001, are drawn from Serena Williams with Daniel Paisner, *Queen of the Court* (London: Simon & Schuster, 2009); Tennis Advocate, "The Fiery Darts of Indian Wells," https://www.youtube.com/watch?v=Yv6rAejg hjA; "Serena Williams v. Kim Clijsters Indian Wells Final Highlights," https://www.youtube.com/watch?v=Wfy30yDE-bE; Alexandre Sokolowski, "March 17, 2001: The Day After Serena Williams Won Indian Wells after Controversy," 17 Mar 2022, https://www.tennismajors.com/wta-tour-news/march-17-2001-the-day-serena-williams-won-indian-wells-after-controversy-327738.html; Selena Roberts, "Serena Wins as the Boos Pour Down," *New York Times*, 18 Mar 2001, https://www.nytimes.com/2001/03/18/sports/tennis-serena-williams-wins-as-the-boos-pour-down.html; Doug Smith, "Williams' Father Says Booing Was Racially Motivated," 28 Mar 2001, http://usatoday30.usatoday.com/sports/tennis/stories/2001-03-26-williams.htm.

151 *How many people do you know:* "Serena Williams on Booing: 'I'm Just a Kid,'" 18 Mar 2001, https://www.espn.com/tennis/news/2001/0317/1157027.html.

151 *I'm very confident:* "Venus Williams' Father Checks Interviewer during Childhood Interview," https://www.youtube.com/watch?v=rOrL1SACwD0.

156 *I swear to God:* Serena Williams qtd. in Lawrence Donegan, "Serena Williams Is Fined $10,500 for US Open Line Judge Tirade," *The Guardian*, 13 Sep 2009, https://www.theguardian.com/sport/2009/sep/13/serena-williams-tirade-us-open.

157 *As offensive as her outburst is:* Claudia Rankine, *Citizen: An American Lyric* (Minneapolis: Graywolf, 2013), 29.

DIVA REVIVALS

159 *Jomama Jones is a living legend:* Fire & Ink, Inc., http://2009.fireandink.org/jones.html.

161 *I'm a lone star:* Song lyrics from *Lone Star* (2010) album liner notes.

161 *Out on the corner:* All song lyrics quoted in chapter are taken from the program book for the production of *Radiate* at SoHo Rep, Dec 2010–Jan 2011.

164 **"intensive mothering":** In *Cultural Contradictions of Motherhood*, Sharon Hays describes "intensive mothering" as the dominant ideology of motherhood that gained momentum during the closing decade of the twentieth century in the United States. According to Hays, intensive mothering is *a gendered model that advises mothers to expend a tremendous amount of time, energy, and money in raising their children and thereby helps to reproduce the existing gender hierarchy and to contribute, with little social or financial compensation for the mothers who sustain its tenets, to the maintenance of capitalism and the centralized state.* Sharon Hays, *Cultural Contradictions of Motherhood* (New Haven: Yale University Press, 1998), x, 178. Andrea O'Reilly, in *What Do Mothers Need?*, observes, *The forces of neoliberalism and intensive mothering have created the perfect storm for twenty-first century motherhood, as mothers today must do far more work with far less resources.* Andrea O'Reilly, *What Do Mothers Need? Motherhood Activists and Scholars Speak Out on Maternal Empowerment for the 21st Century* (Bradford, ON: Demeter Press, 2012), 44.

164 **back from the darkness:** http://www.danielalexanderjones.com/new-page-27/.

165 **by 1997, I'd packed:** Daniel Alexander Jones and Matthew Glassman, "The Radiant Desire of Jomama Jones," *TDR: The Drama Review* 58.4 (2014): 132.

167 *Like how comets*: Staged interview I conducted with Jomama Jones, Columbia University, New York, 11 April 2016.

167 *She's back*: Jacob Gallagher-Ross, "Jomama Jones Returns to the U.S.A.," *The Village Voice*, 12 Jan 2011, https://www.villagevoice.com/2011/01/12/jomama-jones-returns-to-the-u-s-a/.

167 a series of fictionalized: Details from the fictionalized cover stories in *Jet*, *Black Beat*, and *Rock & Soul* are drawn from http://www.danielalexanderjones.com/new-page-61/.

169 **I arrived at Soho Rep**: My observations about *Radiate* were all taken from the two performances I attended at Soho Rep on 31 Jan 2010 and 14 Jan 2011 and from Salvage Vanguard Theatre's archival video of their production in Austin, Texas, on 5 July 2013.

169 *Anyone living in the West Village*: Program notes, *Radiate*, Soho Rep, 14 Jan 2011.

172 *I feel like I'm a little girl*: "Daniel Alexander Jones Talks about Who (He Thinks) Jomama Is," University of Washington School of Drama, 19 Oct 2017, https://www.youtube.com/watch?v=cXJ8Klc9XyM.

173 *Jomama to me is of another dimension*: Kimmel Center for the Performing Arts, "Jomama Jones Talks *Black Light*," 28 Apr 2017, https://www.kimmelculturalcampus.org/blog/jomama-jones-talks-black-light/.

173 *She is my alter-ego*: Jomama Jones qtd. in Joe Franco, "Jomama Jones: A Force of Nature," *Windy City Times*, 11 Apr 2012, https://windycitytimes.com/m/APPredirect.php?AID=37218.

174 **I'm in a chorus singing**: David Rooney, "On Hiatus from the Swiss Goats," *New York Times*, 6 Jan 2011, https://www.nytimes.com/2011/01/07/theater/reviews/07jomama.html; Jill Dolan, *The Feminist Spectator in Action: Feminist Criticism for the Stage and Screen* (Blasingstoke, Hampshire: Palgrave MacMillan, 2013), 172; Hilton Als, "'The Wire: The Musical' Should Win a Tony," *New Yorker*, 7 June 2012, https://www.newyorker.com/culture/culture-desk/the-wire-the-musical-should-win-a-tony.

175 **This is not our mother's camp**: Esther Newton, *Mother Camp: Female Impersonation in America* (Chicago: University of Chicago, 1979).

175 **Soho Rep posted a video**: Soho Rep, "Jomama Explains Her Diva Influences," 3 Dec 2010, https://www.youtube.com/watch?v=KyX8QpfX3AM. All quotes from the video.

175 *Jones didn't use Jomama*: Als, "'The Wire: The Musical.'"

177 *what was and what if*: Alondra Nelson, "Introduction: Future Texts," *Social Text* 71, 20.2 (2002): 4.

177 *terrestrial insurrection*: Kandia Crazy Horse, "Space Oddities," *Offbeat*, (July 2008), 26.

178 *to make the costume into your own*: Joshua Gamson, *The Fabulous Sylvester: The Legend, The Music, The Seventies in San Francisco* (New York: Picador, 2005), 146.

178 *a mix of popular icons*: D. A. Jones and Glassman, "The Radiant Desire of Jomama Jones," 133.

179 *I just remember a posture*: Program notes, *Radiate*, Soho Rep, 14 Jan 2011.

179 *a graceful fusion*: Ernest Hardy, "Liner Notes," *Lone Star*.

180 *In a stellar instant*: Jones and Glassman, "The Radiant Desire of Jomama Jones," 134.

181 *a spiritual mother for the moment*: Naveen Kumar, "Jomama Jones Is a Spir-

itual Mother for the Moment in *Black Light*," *Towleroad*, 10 Oct 2018, https://www.towleroad.com/2018/10/jomama-jones/.

182 *a revival for turbulent times*: *Black Light* promotional materials, Public Theater, 2015.

182 *Ma Rainey would pitch a tent*: Inside the Diva's Studio: Deborah Paredez Interviews Jomama Jones, New York University, 28 Mar 2013.

183 *One of the things that I felt*: Staged interview I conducted with Jomama Jones, Columbia University, 11 Apr 2016.

DIVA PORTALS

185 *a body-soakin' fusion*: Adele Bertei, *Why Labelle Matters* (Austin: University of Texas Press, 2021), 110.

186 *We really treated it like a band*: Nona Hendryx interviewed by Ann Powers, "Labelle Was Always More Than a Lady," *Los Angeles Times*, 12 Oct 2008, https://www.latimes.com/archives/la-xpm-2008-oct-12-ca-labelle12-story.html.

187 *There are few groups that are as important*: "Jomama Explains Her Diva Influences," Soho Rep FEED, 3 Dec 2010, https://www.youtube.com/watch?v=KyX8QpfX3AM.

187 *Labelle sang the opening aria*: Bertei, *Why Labelle Matters*, xii.

187 *In fact, it was the Met's own financial crisis*: Peter Clark, "Technology in Troubled Times," https://www.metopera.org/discover/articles/technology-in-troubled-times/.

189 *Ford to City*: "Ford to City: Drop Dead," *New York Daily News*, 30 Oct 1975.

189 *Within moments of constraint*: Francesca Royster, "Funk, Feminism, and the Politics of Flight and Fight," *American Studies* 52.4 (2013): 77–78.

189 *that sonic rage of love*: Bertei, *Why Labelle Matters*, 119.

191 **Let's go to the Met**: My reconstruction of New York City in 1974 and of Labelle's concert performance at the Met, which aims for historical accuracy, relies upon the following sources: Samuel R. Delaney, *Times Square Red, Time Square Blue* (New York: New York University Press, 2001); Patti Labelle's autobiography written with Laura B. Randolph, *Don't Block the Blessings: Revelations of a Lifetime*; email correspondence with Moira Hodgson and Margo Jefferson; reviews in *Rolling Stone*, *Village Voice*, *Melody Maker*, and *Newsweek*; advertisement in *Village Voice*; Adele Bertei's *Why Labelle Matters*; Wikipedia entry on Butterfly McQueen, https://en.wikipedia.org/wiki/Butterfly_McQueen; Kyna Leski, "The Genesis of the Metropolitan Opera House Chandeliers: How Accident and Intention Come to Light," https://kynaleski.medium.com/genesis-the-chandeliers-of-the-metropolitan-opera-house-2090ee74690e; interviews in the documentary, *Patti Labelle Biography—Intimate Portrait*, https://www.youtube.com/watch?v=TPgd25juF-s; and Nell Greenfield Boyce, "Astronomers Strike Gravitational Gold in Colliding Neutron Stars," National Public Radio, 16 Oct 2017, https://www.npr.org/sections/thetwo-way/2017/10/16/557557544/astronomers-strike-gravitational-gold-in-colliding-neutron-stars.

192 *Village broads with narrow hips*: Audre Lorde, "A Poem for a Poet," *Cables to Rage* (London: Paul Breman, 1970), 20.

198 *Passing stranger!*: Walt Whitman, "To a Stranger," https://poets.org/poem/stranger.

201 *your body has become not yours*: Whitman, "To a Stranger."

EPILOGUE

206 ***The tomb . . . my death-warrant***: Gaetano Donizetti, *Lucia di Lammermoor*, libretto Salvadore Cammarano, 1835. All subsequent quotes from the opera are from this libretto.

208 ***I used to like to challenge myself***: Natalie Dessay in an interview with Rhiannon Giddens, *Aria Code*, "Breaking Mad: Donizetti's *Lucia di Lammermoor*," WNYC Studios, 25 Aug 2021, https://www.wnycstudios.org/podcasts/aria-code/episodes/aria-code-donizetti-lucia-di-lammermoor-natalie-dessay.

208 ***She ornamented her final aria***: Michael Andor Brodeur, "A Thoroughly Modern Meltdown in Met's Re-Imagined *Lucia di Lammermoor*," *Washington Post*, 24 Apr 2022, https://www.washingtonpost.com/arts-entertainment/2022/04/24/met-opera-lucia-di-lammermoor-review/.

209 ***Started writing in this book***: All letter excerpts in this chapter are from my own personal collection of letters sent to me from my Tía Lucia Bustillo from 2000 to 2009.

210 ***Carmen dies, . . . but, oh, her arias!***: Susan Leonardi and Rebecca Pope, *The Diva's Mouth: Body, Voice, Prima Donna Politics* (New Brunswick, NJ: Rutgers University Press, 1996), 16.

Illustration Credits

123 **Defying gravity:** 1992, National Museum of American History.
129 **Holding the frame:** 1995, Michelle Boyd, author's personal collection.
133 **Re-soled and polished:** 2021, Deborah Paredez, author's personal collection.
140 **Diva Girl Mad Libs Erasure Poem: A History Lesson:** 2022, Deborah Paredez, original art by author.
146 **Serena and Venus gleaming amidst the blinding flashes:** 23 August 1997, *New York Daily News* Archives/Getty Images.
155 **Diva Girl Mad Libs Erasure Poem: You Go, Girl! Part Two:** 2022, Deborah Paredez, original art by author.
158 **First tennis lesson:** 2011, Deborah Paredez, author's personal collection.
163 **Jomama delivering her diva lessons:** 2009, Deborah Paredez, author's personal collection.
163 **Jomama nurturing an admiring young fan:** 2009, Deborah Paredez, author's personal collection.
166 **Jomama radiates:** 2011, Nisha Sondhe, courtesy of Daniel Alexander Jones.
174 **Jomama and her Sweet Peaches galloping ahead:** 2011, Nisha Sondhe, courtesy of Daniel Alexander Jones.
181 **Jomama in *Black Light*:** 2017, Deborah Paredez, author's personal collection.
188 **Labelle in silver:** 1975, Gijsbert Hanekroot/Redferns/Getty Images.
200 **Labelle in concert:** 1975, Chris Walker/WireImage/Getty Images.
210 **Sparkling chandelier at the Met:** 2022, Deborah Paredez, author's personal collection.

Index

Page numbers in italic refer to illustrations.

divas
  celebrities vs., 13
  college class on, 27–28
  evolution of, 25, 27
  evolution of term, 9
  and ideas of freedom, 10–11
  interest in, 9–10
  origins of terms, 13
"Divas: Loud, Proud, and Fashionable"
    (Heller), 97
"Divas in Metaphor, Divas in Crisis,
    Divas in Life" (Klein), 102
Diva's Mouth, The (Leonardi and Pope),
    19
Diva Starz Dolls, 145–47
Diva Studies (Alexander), 102
Divine, 14–16, *15*, 81–91, *85*, 175
Dobbs, Mattiwilda, 187
Dolan, Jill, 174
"dolce suono, Il" (The Sweet Sound),
    206–7
Dominguez, Bonnie, 136
Donizetti, Gaetano, 206
"Do Right Woman, Do Right Man,"
    96
"Downhearted Blues," 20
"Down the Aisle (The Wedding Song),"
    185
drag, 172–73
Dreaming of You (Selena), 100, 101
"Dueling Divas" concert, 25
duets, 73, 130–31
Dunaway, Faye, 25
Dunes Motel, 87
Durie, Jo, 150

Ecker, Richard, 186
Edie Brickell & New Bohemians, 105
Ed Sullivan Show, The, 62, 66
El Carnario, 117
"Electrify," 169
EleVen, 135
"Endless Summertime," 161–62
Entertainment Weekly, 25
Epstein, Matthew, 19
"Ese Hombre," 125–26
Essex, Andrew, 25
Estefan, Gloria, 3, 109, 115, 116
Evert, Chris, 136, 142
"Everybody Loves the Sunshine," 162

Factory, The, 86
Faludi, Susan, 97, 99
Fame (Grace Jones), 14
Fania All-Stars, 120
Fear of Flying (Jong), 113
feeling brown, 55
Félix, Maria, 40
Female Trouble (film), 86
feminism, 19–20, 92–116
"Feminism: It's All About me" (Bella-
    fante), 113
Fiddler on the Roof, 43
Fire and Ink Cotillion, 159, 161
Fogerty, John, 60, 61
"Fool in Love, A," 59
Ford, Gerald, 189
Ford to City: Drop Dead, 189
Foreman, George, 122
Franklin, Aretha, 18, 22, 24, 92–116, *95*
Franklin, C. L., 96
freedom, 10–11, 68–69
French Open tennis tournament, 153
Friedan, Betty, 112
Frozen, 28

Gamboa, Harry, Jr., 87
Garcia, Cindy, 127
"Ghetto (In My Mind)," 159
Gibson, Althea, 151
Girlfriends (television program), 137
girlhood, 142–44
Girl Power, 142
Glee (television program), 53
Godzilla, 163
golden-age musicals, 43
"Gone Platinum" Barbie, 144–45
Gonna Take a Miracle (Labelle), 186
Graf, Steffi, 153
Graham, Martha, 177
Granada Homes, 34
Green, Juanita, 20–21
Griffin, Farah Jasmine, 18, 19
Gronk, 82, 87
"Guantanamera," 120–21
"Gypsy Moths," 186

Hairspray (film), 86–87, 175
Halverson, Bobby, 165
Hannah Montana (television program),
    137